Cambridge Elements ≡

Elements in Politics and Society in Latin America
edited by
Maria Victoria Murillo
Columbia University
Tulia G. Falleti
University of Pennsylvania
Juan Pablo Luna
The Pontifical Catholic University of Chile
Andrew Schrank
Brown University

CONSERVATIVES AGAINST THE TIDE

The Rise of the Argentine PRO in Comparative Perspective

Gabriel Vommaro
Universidad de San Martin, Escuela Interdisciplinaria de Altos Estudios Sociales

CAMBRIDGE
UNIVERSITY PRESS

Shaftesbury Road, Cambridge CB2 8EA, United Kingdom

One Liberty Plaza, 20th Floor, New York, NY 10006, USA

477 Williamstown Road, Port Melbourne, VIC 3207, Australia

314–321, 3rd Floor, Plot 3, Splendor Forum, Jasola District Centre,
New Delhi – 110025, India

103 Penang Road, #05–06/07, Visioncrest Commercial, Singapore 238467

Cambridge University Press is part of Cambridge University Press & Assessment,
a department of the University of Cambridge.

We share the University's mission to contribute to society through the pursuit of
education, learning and research at the highest international levels of excellence.

www.cambridge.org
Information on this title: www.cambridge.org/9781009418249

DOI: 10.1017/9781009418256

First published 2023

A catalogue record for this publication is available from the British Library.

ISBN 978-1-009-41824-9 Paperback
ISSN 2515-5253 (online)
ISSN 2515-5245 (print)

Conservatives against the Tide

The Rise of the Argentine PRO in Comparative Perspective

Elements in Politics and Society in Latin America

DOI: 10.1017/9781009418256
First published online: June 2023

Gabriel Vommaro
*Universidad de San Martin, Escuela Interdisciplinaria
de Altos Estudios Sociales*

Author for correspondence: Gabriel Vommaro, gvommaro@unsam.edu.ar

Abstract: This Element in the Elements series addresses the success of conservative parties in nonauthoritarian contexts in contemporary Latin America. It places the core case of Argentina's Republican Proposal (PRO) party in comparison with Argentina's Recrear, Colombia's Democratic Center (CD) party, and Bolivia's Social Democratic Movement (MDS) in an effort to understand their differing degrees of success in adverse circumstances. Based on long-term research carried out using a variety of methods, this Element shows that the PRO's success has been driven by three factors: programmatic innovation by personalistic leaders; organizational mobilization of both core and noncore constituencies; and elite fear of the "Venezuela model."

Keywords: right-wing parties, political parties, Latin America, moral panic, political sociology

ISBNs: 9781009418249 (PB), 9781009418256 (OC)
ISSNs: 2515-5253 (online), 2515-5245 (print)

Contents

Introduction

Faced with the crisis of traditional parties in the context of the "unfreezing" of the post–World War II frozen party system (Gidron & Ziblatt, 2019), new parties have serious difficulties in building solid foundations that allow them to endure over time. Scholars of Latin American politics have pointed out the difficulties of party building in the region (Levitsky, Loxton, & Van Dyck, 2016) and of maintaining party vibrancy (Rosenblatt, 2018), as well as the transience of many Latin American political parties (Coppedge, 1998). Investing in two types of costly resources crucial for party building, organizational and ideational (Cyr, 2017), is uncommon in a terrain of personalist vehicles and flash parties with little capacity for coordination and interest aggregation (Luna et al., 2021). The scenario is even more grim for conservative parties.[1] Only four of the eleven successful parties – belonging to three countries – documented by Levitsky, Loxton, and Van Dyck's study (2016) are conservative: Democratas (Brazil), Unión Demócrata Independiente (Independent Democratic Union, UDI) and Renovación Nacional (National Renovation, RN) (Chile), and Alianza Republicana Nacionalista (National Republican Alliance, ARENA) (El Salvador).[2] All of them were born in the early 1980s, in authoritarian contexts. Existing theory on conservative-party building in Latin America (Loxton, 2016; 2021) maintains that under these adverse conditions, only parties with authoritarian roots managed to be successful. In this context, one of the novelties of Argentine politics after the economic crisis of 2001–2, when unemployment reached 21.5 percent of the economically active population in the main urban agglomerates and more than half the population fell into poverty, is particularly surprising: that novel event was the formation of a conservative party that was not only successful, according to the parameters of the available theory (Levitsky, Loxton, & Van Dyck, 2016: 36), but also probably one of the most successful new right-wing parties in Latin America.[3] Propuesta

---

[1] "Conservative parties are defined here as parties whose core constituencies are upper social and economic strata but that mobilize multiclass electoral support in a common political project" (Middlebrook, 2000: 3).

[2] Since the beginning of the third wave of democratization (Huntington, 1991), there were only 11 successful parties out of more than 300 new parties in 18 Latin American countries (Levitsky, Loxton, & Van Dyck, 2016: 5).

[3] I opt for the term "conservative party" because it is the most unequivocally related to the definition I adopt in this Element: a party whose core constituency is found in the upper strata and economic elites. In some passages, for convenience of writing, I use the term "right-wing party" as a synonym. Likewise, by "new right-wing parties" I mean parties born after the third wave of democratization (Huntington, 1991). The PRO survived the defeat of its leader and completed five legislative elections with more than 10 percent of the vote, if we count the 2013 legislative elections (in which it obtained part of its vote share in a subnational coalition in the province of Buenos Aires); in 2023 it will have competed in five election cycles, and it remains the dominant party in a coalition.

Republicana (Republican Proposal, PRO) was led by a businessman and formed by a combination of traditional politicians (members of minor conservative parties, members of the Unión Cívica Radical (Radical Civic Union, UCR), and members of the Justicialist, or Peronist, party), newcomers from the business world, and elite nongovernmental organizations (NGOs). The UCR and the Peronist party were the main Argentine parties of the twentieth century. The UCR was born at the beginning of that century, Peronism after World War II. Both were founded as mass movements structured around a personalist leader; Peronism became a workers' party, while the UCR took root in the urban middle classes. In the same vein, the PRO was born as a party based on a personalist leadership, although it later carried out a successful party-building process, based on its roots in the city of Buenos Aires. In 2007, the PRO was elected to head the government of the city of Buenos Aires, which it still controls today. Starting in local government, it adopted a more flexible approach to social and economic conservatism and a hardline approach to crime. In the 2015 presidential elections, the Cambiemos (Let's Change) coalition, led by the PRO and made up of the traditional UCR, the Coalición Cívica (Civic Coalition), and other minor partners, managed to defeat Peronism electorally, after a decade of electoral predominance by the Frente para la Victoria (Front for Victory, FPV), a left-of-center coalition built around the Peronist party and led by Néstor Kirchner and Cristina Fernández de Kirchner. Cambiemos had a poor economic performance in office and failed to be re-elected in the 2019 presidential election. However, the PRO remained competitive and vibrant; it again led a winning coalition in the 2021 mid-term elections and prepared to run competitively in the 2023 presidential election.

Given the challenging context for party building in Latin America (Levitsky, Loxton, & Van Dyck, 2016), the success of the PRO is also surprising for other reasons. Partisan rightists in Argentina have historically been quite weak (Di Tella, 1971–2; Gibson, 1996), and the partisan right have faced structural problems that have impeded their ability to mobilize secondary electorates, especially in the lower classes, and thus become competitive (Gibson, 1992; 1996; Loxton, 2021). Free-market programs have rigid limits in confronting this challenge, especially in highly unequal societies where redistribution is required (Luna & Rovira Kaltwasser, 2014). Also, the broadening of social consensus around same-sex marriage and the expansion of sexual and gender-identity rights in early twenty-first-century Latin America (Biroli & Caminotti, 2021) left conservative sectors in the minority in terms of the cultural agenda. In this vein, in his study on the birth of conservative parties in Europe, Ziblatt (2017) refers to the "conservative dilemma," a term that describes this tension between defending elite interests and the need to play the electoral game and conquer majorities. Finally, the PRO case is surprising because it is a party without authoritarian roots. This contradicts expectations about the development of conservative parties, which holds that only authoritarian successor parties (ASP) can be successful because they are uniquely able to make use of the otherwise-inaccessible party-building resources that stem from the authoritarian period (Loxton, 2016; 2021). The PRO constitutes a deviant case for this existent theory (Seawright & Gerring, 2008). Deviant cases allow us to identify the limits of a theory and can permit us to identify factors left unaddressed – in this case, the success of a conservative party that came into being in a nonauthoritarian context.

What explains the PRO's success in that context? In what follows I identify three primary factors that explain conservative-party formation in nonauthoritarian Argentina. First, programmatic innovation allowed the PRO to reach beyond the niche of right-wing voters in a context adverse to a conservative social consensus; second, the construction of organizational links with core and noncore constituencies gave it social roots, provided it with cadres and militants, and contributed to its persistence in times when the FPV was electorally dominant; and finally, the strategic association of Peronism with the threat of the "Venezuela model" was a tactic that allowed the PRO to build an "epic narrative" and a sense of urgency that could mobilize its core constituency. The first two factors are related to how parties function internally, especially how organizational resources (Panebianco, 1989) built by party leaders serve to cement support from their core and secondary constituencies. These are factors that developed over time. They began in the early stages of PRO party building and were carefully replicated and maintained; they are also costly and require sustained support from at least some party leaders (Cyr, 2017). The third factor refers to the strategic use of a moral panic (Cohen, 1972), associated with fear of redistribution, threats to private property, and the empowerment of personalistic leaders who hinder elite access to government (Durand & Silva, 1998), thus triggering the fears of the conservative electoral core. Through an epic narrative based on confronting this threat, leaders accelerate hesitant support and mobilize sectors that are apathetic toward the party.

According to my argument, conservative parties do not depend fundamentally on authoritarian contexts to obtain the organizational and ideational resources that are essential to their success. Applying this argument to the case of the PRO shows that these resources can be the result of organizational work by the party and its leaders. Certainly, these resources are costly to obtain and difficult to maintain over time. That explains why the PRO is one of the few successful cases of conservative parties without authoritarian roots. Nevertheless, the case shows that resources internalized as party assets allow political groups to both: (1) grow in programmatic contexts that are adverse for conservative parties, that is, in contexts marked by normative consensuses adverse to conservative ideas (in the cultural field) and to the interests of the conservative core constituency (in economic issues); and (2) maintain cohesion in moments of setbacks (electoral defeats, departure of the leader). Likewise, the case of the PRO confirms that entrepreneurial resources become central for conservative parties both in organizational and ideational terms (Gibson, 1996; Loxton, 2021). However, it also adds an important nuance: these resources are obtained from party work, and not through "outsourcing" to corporations (Barndt, 2014) or only from direct support from business associations. Likewise, in these nonauthoritarian contexts, there is considerable polarization and political conflict, and conservative parties can find sources of cohesion in the activation of "moral panics" (Cohen, 1972) associated with their political adversary. As a result, they do not require contexts of counterinsurgency wars to take root (Loxton, 2021).

Certainly, context matters. The collapse of the party system provides a favorable opportunity for the formation of new political groups (Seawright, 2012). Likewise, the absence of a competitive conservative party leaves room for a new alternative to emerge. Yet context is not enough to explain the success or failure of conservative forces in party building. In addition to explaining the surprising success of PRO, in this Element I analyze another conservative-party-building attempt in Argentina. At the same time that the PRO was emerging, Recrear was trying to stake out a place in national politics with a more rigid neoliberal platform. Recrear was a coalition between former leaders of the UCR and provincial conservative parties. After a promising start with a third-place finish in the 2003 presidential elections, Recrear entered a phase of internal disputes that led to its decline. The PRO and Recrear, both offspring of the 2001–2 crisis, embarked on parallel paths under similar conditions. The failure of Recrear offers a fruitful opportunity for comparison and allows me to show the importance of party-level factors in explaining its success or failure in party building.

The demands on conservative-party building are certainly higher in non-authoritarian contexts, when external resources are scarcer. The armed forces lose relevance as an organizational support for new political options; the fear of armed subversion as a source of cohesion of conservative forces is no longer on the agenda; accordingly, economic elites have less incentive to support political organizations that defend their interests. In order to show how my argument travels to other contexts, I also offer empirical illustrations of other cases of Latin American conservative parties that did not rely on resources rooted in authoritarian legacies and had uneven levels of success. The first example is the Centro Democrático (CD) in Colombia; although less successful than the PRO, it managed to build a solid electoral vehicle but was heavily dependent on its leader, Álvaro Uribe (Gamboa Gutiérrez, 2019). It is yet unclear whether the CD will survive severe setbacks such as an electoral failure or Uribe's exit from politics. A second negative case is found in the Movimiento Democrático Social (MDS), the largest-scale attempt to build a conservative party in Bolivia to date. The MDS never managed to expand from its stronghold in the eastern province of Santa Cruz, because it was unable to develop solid organizational and ideational resources in that region that would make it attractive as a national conservative option (Eaton, 2016).

Sections of This Element

This Element is organized as follows. The first section lays out the research design and theoretical argument. The following four sections are focused on the main case. Section 2 contextualizes the birth of the PRO as set against the recent history of conservative parties in Argentina. The subsequent three sections address the three factors identified in my explanation of conservative parties' success in nonauthoritarian contexts. In the third section I analyze programmatic innovation. In the fourth section I consider the organizational mechanisms that allowed the PRO to mobilize its core constituency as well as establish relationships with noncore constituencies. The fifth section discusses the "moral panic" exploited by the conservative political mobilization. The sixth section deals with the interactions between these three factors, both in terms of their feedback and of the ways in which they can be neutralized. The seventh section tests my argument using the case of Recrear in Argentina. In the last section, I draw conclusions about conservative-party building in Latin America that help to establish a comparative analysis research agenda. To that end I offer empirical illustrations of the CD in Colombia and the MDS in Bolivia.

1 Research Design and Theoretical Approach

In this section, I first describe the case selection and research design. Then, I clarify my theoretical approach. I identify the gaps in the existing theory on conservative-party building, which maintains that party building is grounded in resources provided by authoritarian roots, and I extrapolate upon my three-factor model, explaining conservative-party-building success in democratic contexts as a way to contribute to filling those gaps.

1.1 Case Selection and Research Design

In this Element, I analyze the PRO as a core case in order to build my theory (Ragin, 1994). The PRO is a conservative party that has managed to develop the resources to be successful in a nonauthoritarian context. It is probably one of the most successful conservative parties in Latin America and is also a deviant case (Seawright & Gerring, 2008) in ASP theory. Its surprising nature makes it very useful for the development of new explanations. According to ASP theory, only conservative parties with authoritarian roots can obtain the resources necessary for successful party development. The Argentine case provides a propitious example with which to study the factors that explain the formation of conservative parties in nonauthoritarian contexts. The successful trajectory of PRO can also be compared to the failed one of the conservative party Recrear, which tried to take root under similar conditions but was not able to consolidate as PRO did. In 2007, PRO leader Mauricio Macri became the head of the government of the city of Buenos Aires, a position that the PRO still held at the time of publication. The government of the city of Buenos Aires allowed the PRO to obtain resources to feed its party structure and consolidate a brand based on management and problem-solving. With ups and downs, the PRO has grown in electoral terms since 2007, expanding its position in other districts of the country, and as a result of its coalitional strategy, it ran candidates in local elections across the nation in 2015.

A second conservative party, Recrear, emerged in similar conditions but obtained very different results. Although Recrear initially arose as the most promising conservative party in the wake of the 2001–2 crisis, it fell apart shortly thereafter. In its formative years, Recrear had more resources than the PRO. Its leader, Ricardo López Murphy, was a renowned economist with extensive participation in the UCR, and a prominent member of Fundación de Investigaciones Económicas Latinoamericanas (Latin American Economic Research Foundation, FIEL), a neoliberal think tank. Although it grew rapidly and came in third place in the 2003 presidential elections, Recrear began a steep decline shortly thereafter; it went into crisis before merging with the PRO in 2010. A good part of the small provincial conservative groups that had seen in López Murphy the possibility of finally building a competitive national conservative party redirected their hopes toward the party led by Macri.

Studying the processes of party building requires extended observation of the organizational life of a party over time. A longer-term view makes it possible to combine a dynamic approach that contemplates the evolution of the party's resources with a static approach that describes the characteristics of the party and its leaders at a precise moment. It also requires a combination of methods and materials that account for the different dimensions of party life: the characteristics of leaders and militants, public speeches by leadership, party territorial implantation, and electoral performance. Examining a collective actor by aggregating the characteristics of its members is also challenging, as it implies combining an analysis of the resources and the points of view of individuals with analysis of those of the entire organization. To address this challenge, my study combines a survey-based description of leaders' features with a process tracing of the evolution of the characteristics of party organizational and ideational resources. Another challenge is the scale of analysis. Studying a party at the national level can minimize the subnational heterogeneities of a party's life, its leaders, and its local roots. Starting from the local level and especially from the district of origin, often a party stronghold, permits one to observe the party's early development, and then extend the observation to other districts. This is even more useful in the case of centralized parties such as the PRO, whose leading coalition is still highly concentrated in its stronghold. The city of Buenos Aires has been chosen here as the main district for the study of PRO party building, because the party built its program and its main organizational resources in this district. Moreover, most of the Cambiemos government cadres at the national level in 2015, and in other districts (at the subnational level), originated in the capital city.

In line with these challenges, the data comes from longer-term research (2010–19) on the PRO's party-building efforts – in organizational, sociological, and programmatic terms – in the city of Buenos Aires; its territorial expansion strategies in other districts; and its transformation in recent years. The first stage of the research consisted of an in-depth quantitative-qualitative study of the social anchors, ideas, and activities of PRO political cadres and activists in the city of Buenos Aires (Morresi & Vommaro, 2014; Vommaro & Morresi, 2014; Vommaro, Morresi, & Bellotti, 2015). This work included two surveys (2011 and 2014–15) of PRO leaders, in-depth interviews with PRO leaders and activists (forty-five), and a review of press and partisan archives, as well as ethnographic description of rallies and meetings. The sample size of the 2011 survey is n=52, out of a population N=76 (68.4 percent). The population includes the mayor's cabinet ministers, the secretaries and undersecretaries of each ministry, the national deputies representing the city of Buenos Aires, and the deputies of the local legislature. The sample included six ministers (out of nine), three secretaries (out of five), twenty-two undersecretaries (out of thirty-one), four national deputies (out of seven), and seventeen legislators (out of twenty-four). The 2014–15 sample size is n=50 out of a population of ninety-eight cases (51 percent). In this case, the population comprises legislative positions entirely: senators and national deputies representing the city of Buenos Aires, deputies of the local legislature, and community members of the fifteen communes of the district. The sample comprised one senator (out of two), nine national deputies (out of eleven), sixteen legislators (out of twenty-five), and twenty-five communal deputies (out of sixty). I then extended the study by comparing PRO political elites in the capital city of Buenos Aires with political elites based in two other cities: Quilmes, which is located in the Buenos Aires Metropolitan Area, and Pergamino, in the heart of the agrarian hub of Buenos Aires province. The sample size is n=45 out of a population of fifty-eight cases (77.6 percent). In this case, the population comprises the secretaries of the mayor and the deputies of the local legislature. The sample consisted of twenty-eight secretaries and undersecretaries (out of thirty-six) and seventeen legislators (out of twenty-two). Finally, I surveyed PRO deputies and national senators (2017 survey). The sample size of the 2017 survey is n=35, out of a population N=65 (53.8 percent). All surveys followed the snowball sampling method, which allows for surveying hard-to-access populations such as political elites. I supplemented this technique with a quota selection. In all surveys, the sample was selected in such a way as to maintain a certain proportion regarding gender and position. Although the samples were small and unrepresentative, the results are both suggestive and consistent with what I found elsewhere in my study. The surveys were mostly administered in person, and only in a marginal number of cases via an online platform. The questionnaires included questions on: (1) basic data allowing social identification of the members of the political elites (sex, date of birth, place of residence, educational level, educational training establishments, family composition, profession, and parents' educational level); (2) occupational data (other current occupations, last three occupations linked or not linked to politics before accessing the first position held in the period); (3) political and party trajectory (year and organization of entry into politics, parents' political activity, previous or present affiliation to other party/parties, party affiliation, party position); (4) relations with politics and with the party (party activities that take the most time, reasons for approaching the political organization from which they reached the position, participation in and views on other associations: social movements, trade unions, think tanks, civil, religious associations, etc.); (5) political and cultural opinions and practices (ideological positioning on the left–right scale, religious beliefs and practices, definitions of democracy, and political attitudes regarding issues on the political, economic, social, and cultural agenda, with positioning on a scale of 1–5). These surveys also allow us to compare PRO elites with those who came from Recrear and had only recently become PRO members at the time the surveys were conducted.[4]

I also conducted interviews with PRO leaders from other provinces, especially from Córdoba, Tucumán, and Santiago del Estero. This data was combined with party documents and press archives to reconstruct the PRO

---

[4] For more information on survey design and implementation, please contact the author.

party-building process beyond its stronghold, its strategies for expanding the party to the interior of the country, and its evolution in programmatic terms, as well as those of its territorial organization and electoral strategies.

In the case of Recrear in Argentina, I conducted interviews with key informants (partisan leaders and scholars) as well as a series of in-depth interviews with former partisan leaders. I analyzed its party program using the Manifesto Project Database.[5] In both cases, I consulted the archives of the major national media outlets to reconstruct the critical junctures in the construction of party organization, programmatic innovations, and party leaders' public discourse.

1.2 Explaining the Success of Conservative Parties: Existing Theories

Conservative groups have faced substantial obstacles on the path to successful party building. One of these obstacles is structural and is due to the sociopolitical characteristics of these parties (Gibson, 1996; Luna, 2010; Loxton, 2016). As noted, the core constituency of conservative parties is comprised of the upper classes and economic elites (Gibson, 1996). However, as Gibson (1992; 1996) has pointed out, in addition to their core constituency, right-wing parties must attract secondary or noncore constituencies to become electorally viable. Ziblatt's (2017) "conservative dilemma" describes this tension between defending elite interests and the need to play the electoral game and conquer majorities. Given this, a conservative party is the major vehicle for elites to unite with other social sectors in a common political project. The challenge for emergent conservative parties is thus twofold: on the one hand, they must attract and mobilize social and economic elites, in some cases getting them to abandon or add to their previous political preferences; on the other hand, they must seek out electoral support in other social sectors, among voters who have previously supported other parties (Holland, 2013; Loxton, 2016). The construction of appropriate organizational mechanisms for these two tasks is thus an important factor in explaining the success of conservative parties.

The mobilization of secondary constituencies means attracting a wider electorate than the party's core voters, who tend to be small in number, in order to build a competitive force. As Gibson argues, "the study of conservative political action in democratic politics is, therefore, the study of the construction of polyclassist coalitions" (1992: 15) Thus, the study of right-wing party building must consider the strategies these parties have used to attract voters, including lower-class voters. In large part, as we will see, in this case they did so by including local leaders from weakened traditional parties; these leaders provided them

---

[5] See https://manifesto-project.wzb.eu/.

with connections with lower-class voters. In programmatic terms, the linkages with noncore constituencies, far from being associated with class interests, "are built in part by weakening class-based solidarity and replacing it with other sources of collective identity" (Gibson, 1992: 19), such as problem-solving by management or hardline security (*mano dura*) discourses. The construction of programmatic appeals that allow conservative parties to mobilize upper classes and economic elites on the one hand and noncore constituencies on the other hand thus becomes a critical issue for new parties that want to challenge established ones.

The building of these programmatic appeals is more critical when the traditional program of the Right does not generate a broad social consensus. In such cases, persisting with traditional positions may consolidate a party's roots in its electoral core, but may also lead it to remain a niche party. In the context of the post-neoliberal consensus in Latin America, the new rightist coalitions had to strengthen themselves in the midst of dominant left-wing parties or, at least, of government agendas traditionally contrary to those of the Right.[6] These agendas included, for example, redistribution and the reduction of inequality (Luna & Rovira Kaltwasser, 2014) and the rights to sexual and gender equality and freedom traditionally opposed by conservative sectors. The crisis of the neoliberal consensus gave way to an agenda dominated by the search for higher levels of social justice and popular participation in the democratic process (Levitsky & Roberts, 2011). The regulatory power of the state was once again at the center of the dominant political orientations. The expansion and universalization of social policies by means of massive cash-transfer programs to informal sectors occupied a large part of public budgets (Garay, 2016; Pribble, 2013). The programmatic issue then became a critical point for the conservative parties. The same challenge emerged with respect to the cultural agenda. The broadening of the social consensus around gay marriage and the expansion of sexual and gender-identity rights (Biroli & Caminotti, 2021) led some right-wing parties to abandon traditional conservative positions, even against the inclinations of part of their constituencies, in order not to lose competitiveness among secondary constituencies.[7]

---

[6] In the 1990s, most of the region embraced neoliberalism ("Washington Consensus-led") to the extent that even labor-based parties such as that of Peronism adopted market reforms (Stokes, 2001). These policies, which included the privatization of state-owned enterprises, deregulation of financial and labor markets, drastic reduction of protections for domestic industries, and fiscal deficits, met with broad social consensus at the outset. Later, when these policies were in crisis, the early 2000s saw a "pink tide," marked by the rise of progressive governments and a reaction against neoliberalism.

[7] Certainly, the conservative approach to the cultural agenda is context dependent. As we will see in the case of Colombia, in cases where progressive consensuses in this field were not strong enough, conservative parties also sought to represent the cultural backlash against advances in reproductive, gender, and sexual-orientation rights.

Given these obstacles, the importance of authoritarian roots has become a central element in recent theories on party building. This has led some authors to argue that the way Latin American democracy functions discourages the formation of successful parties and that, on the contrary, the "ideal contexts" for party building are those of liberalization or competitive authoritarianism (Van Dyck, 2021: 6). In the same vein, the most recent theory available to explain conservative-party formation argues that only ASPs can be successful (Loxton, 2016; 2021). The theory of ASP finds that the fundamental resources for party building for right-wing parties are rooted in authoritarian periods. Specifically, conservative parties can mobilize inheritances from authoritarian periods to face the structural challenge of the construction of a multiclass electoral coalition. According to Loxton (2016), ASPs obtain five resources from their authoritarian roots: organizational infrastructure, providing territorial bases that operate as support networks for the party; privileged ties to economic elites, which allow for more direct and fluid sources of party financing; clientelist networks, offering resources for building a multiclass coalition of support; popular party brands based on the cases of successful dictatorships that have provided goods that the population values (security, order, economic growth); and sources of party cohesion, linked both to the esprit de corps forged in counterinsurgency struggles and to the support of the authoritarian leaders associated with those struggles. He further argues that the importance of authoritarian resources is such that only parties of this type were successful after the third wave of democratization in Latin America.

However, in the wake of the crisis of the neoliberal consensus, the PRO, a non-ASP conservative party, emerged and became competitive, even under adverse circumstances. Moreover, ASPs that had been successful in previous years, such as the Acción Democrática Nacionalista (National Democratic Action, ADN) in Bolivia, collapsed (Cyr, 2017), despite having the resources identified in the ASP model. I argue that these five resources only explain the success of conservative parties in specific conditions, associated with the persistence of authoritarian legacies in voters' identifications and in the public agenda, that is, in the years immediately following authoritarian regimes (the 1980s or 1990s, depending on the country). Under other conditions, the resources described in ASP theory could have other empirical sources. This is the case, for instance, when: (1) programmatic challenges arise due to the weakening of cleavages inherited from the authoritarian period (for Chile, see Huneeus, 2014; Rovira Kaltwasser, 2019); (2) there is a resurgence of the Left and progressive agendas in the economic and cultural fields (Levitsky & Roberts, 2011); and/or (3) many countries experience a collapse of the party system as a result of economic and social crises (Cyr, 2017), as in 2001–2 in Argentina (Torre, 2003).

Finally, even if conflict continues to play a crucial role in the construction of a party's political cohesion, that conflict is not necessarily associated with political violence, the counterrevolutionary struggle and the authoritarian past (Loxton, 2021). The strategic ability to use moral incentives associated with threats in a way that advantages conservative parties is nonetheless relevant, but it may have other empirical manifestations. In my argument, "the Venezuela model" and "gender ideology" – the latter a term used by conservative activists to disqualify demands for sexual diversity rights – emerge as efficient threats to conservative publics; neither necessarily refers to authoritarian roots. The crucial point is the ability of party builders to tap into some threat that is "salient" at that juncture and that allows them to mobilize conservative audiences. The fear of Argentina "becoming another Venezuela," for example, mobilizes a threat (and provokes a moral panic) that is salient to many.

This Element also helps to underscore how party-level studies can contribute to understanding party building. Party-level studies can complement party-systems studies (Mainwaring, 2018; Mainwaring & Scully, 1995) by showing how, under similar conditions, party actors use the ideational and organizational resources at their disposal in a variety of ways and make different bets over time, and how those diverse uses and bets yield different outcomes that have consequences for party life. Certainly, the collapse of party systems generates conditions conducive to the formation of new political groups (Seawright, 2012) by dissolving some existing party brands (Lupu, 2016), allowing the redefinition of political cleavages, and leaving ambitious politicians available (Torre, 2003). But that context is not enough to explain successful party building. In Argentina, two conservative parties emerged from the 2001 crisis, the PRO and Recrear, but only the PRO managed to be successful. To understand these different outcomes, I will open the "black box" of party functioning (Levitsky, 2001).

1.3 Building Successful Conservative Parties in Adverse Times: A Sociopolitical Strategic Approach

To explain how the PRO obtained the necessary resources for its successful party building, I focus on the organizational work of the party and its leaders (Panebianco, 1988; Cyr, 2017; Pérez Bentancur, Piñeiro Rodríguez, & Rosenblatt, 2019). In contrast to arguments that emphasize the causal weight of the institutional context (authoritarian contexts, competitive authoritarianisms, contexts of liberalization, or collapse of the party system), my explanation focuses on factors located at the party level. On the one hand, it looks at the agency of political leaders, that is, how these actors manage to obtain resources for the construction of their party given the conditions; on the other hand, it examines how the organizational mechanisms put in place by leaders contribute to the production and reproduction of party resources (Anria, 2018). I focus on two types of resources, organizational and ideational. These are high-cost resources, but they are also quite durable, allowing parties to survive in difficult times (Cyr, 2017).

The model I propose in this Element draws on studies on the programmatic adaptation of parties (Levitsky, 2001; Burgess, 2003). In line with these works, it is interested in the challenges experienced by parties in an environment hostile to their ideas. Just as the neoliberal challenge of the 1980s and 1990s forced Latin American populist parties to adapt or perish, the post-neoliberal challenge led conservative parties to become more moderate, as in the case of Chilean right-wing parties (Rovira Kaltwasser, 2019) and the PRO in Argentina, or to take available issues and make them part of their party brand (Holland, 2013), as was the case with internal security for the CD in Colombia and problem-solving for the PRO in Argentina. Programmatic innovation has allowed conservative parties to expand their support in adverse contexts and to occupy a definite place in the political competition as a party "owner" of issues that contribute to defining their party brands (Lupu, 2016). Parties' capacity for programmatic innovation is often positively associated with flexible internal structures (Levitsky, 2003) and intense challenges from the economic and social environment (Burgess, 2003). Our Element specifies the range of applicability of these theories to conservative parties and shows that the type of ruling coalition dominant in each party and the division of labor among its members also favor or hinder parties' programmatic flexibility. In the case of the PRO, we will see that programmatic renewal was also favored by the entry of new political personnel who were less committed to the traditional ideas of the conservative groups and who were able to define the program and control the party brand in a centralized manner. On the contrary, this renewal was hindered in the case of Recrear. In that case, the leaders of traditional conservative groups were in the majority and were opposed to making the conservative program more flexible.

My scheme in this Element also joins it to other recent works on the organizational mechanisms that give solidity to party building. Several recent studies have focused on how some successful parties build stable and fluid relationships with their bases, either from the channels of influence of those bases in their internal life (Pérez Bentancur, Piñeiro Rodríguez, & Rosenblatt, 2019) or from the active and permanent participation of social movements in party life (Anria, 2018). These studies analyzed popular-based progressive parties. Yet, we know that parties establish different relationships with different social bases according to the characteristics of these groups and the different contexts in which they act (Gibson, 1996; Luna, 2014; Anria, 2018). The PRO incorporated the leaders of traditional parties to connect it with secondary constituencies traditionally distanced from conservative options (Luna, 2010). This allowed the PRO to carry out the work of broad electoral coalition building, critical in the construction of competitive conservative parties (Gibson, 1996; Luna, 2010; Loxton, 2016). The PRO also managed to mobilize social bases linked to economic elites. These groups usually have an attitude of distance and even distrust toward partisan politics (Gibson, 1996). In most cases they have acted in a coordinated manner in other institutional arenas in which they have managed to influence the government and its policies (Schneider, 2004). On some occasions, as in the Argentine case, economic elites have adopted particularistic and uncoordinated behaviors that involved personalized relationships with politicians rather than organizations, and especially those politicians who were likely to gain power. How does one build relationships with a party's social base when that base is dispersed and does not spontaneously show willingness to participate in party life? My approach specifies the applicability of studies on the construction of social anchors of parties to the case of a conservative party that seeks to attract businessmen and CEOs. It shows, through studying the PRO's linkage with the business world, that parties can create what I call "close-to-the-party organizations" that lower the costs and increase the incentives associated with participation in party life. These organizations manage to attract members of the economic elite through activities adapted to the environments that these groups usually inhabit. The PRO created think tanks and foundations linked to the party that sought to reproduce business social environments (especially exclusive clubs for businesspeople), as well as the activities they carried out in those environments: mentoring of young people and newcomers, social volunteering activities, spiritual retreats to redefine objectives and increase group cohesion. Through these activities, they succeeded in encouraging entrepreneurs and CEOs to participate. They also turned some of them into peer organizers (Han, 2014), which solidified this mobilization work by allocating roles and tasks to new entrants in organizations that were close to the party, and then in government. These supports provided militants and electoral mobilizers in a context of declining party activism (Scarrow, 2000). Likewise, they allowed a new party to create technical cadres that could formulate programs and hold government positions (Cyr, 2017). Finally, they favored the consolidation over time of the support of economic elites, key to the development of conservative parties (Gibson, 1996). My work corroborates the importance of studying informal organizations that give parties roots (Levitsky, 2003) and make party boundaries porous with those of other social milieus (Offerlé, 1987). These linkages are related to the construction of "social worlds of belonging" (Vommaro, 2017) in which parties recruit activists and cadres, develop repertoires of action and discourse, and build their "partisan

environment" (Sawicki, 1997); that is, the set of formal and informal organizations that are not part of the party's organizational chart but are fundamental to its
social roots.

Finally, my argument bridges cultural studies and party theories regarding the
use of threats as resources for partisan mobilization (Gibson, 1996; Middlebrook,
2000; Blee & Creasap, 2010; Wodak, 2015; Ziblatt, 2017). Latin America is
a propitious context for this task. Throughout the second half of the twentieth
century, and particularly during the Cold War, the fear of communism was
a powerful incentive for the mobilization and unity of right-wing partisans in
Latin America (Williams, 2017). However, this threat did not necessarily result in
party building. Before that, in some countries, such as Argentina, Brazil, and
Chile, conservative groups sought other ways of defending the status quo,
generally by violent means such as coups d'état (Di Tella, 1971–2). The years
of the transitions to democracy constituted an interregnum in this mobilization of
threats, prolonged by the long neoliberal decade that reconciled the Right with the
popular vote. In contrast, the years of the "left turn" and the advance of progressive cultural agendas again created conditions for the use of panic as an instrument of political mobilization. The redistributive advances of the "left-turn"
governments triggered threats among the upper strata and economic elites
throughout the region. The "Venezuela model" condensed this threat, as the
Chávez government was the one that had gone furthest in nationalizing companies and controlling markets. This Element contributes to an understanding of the
conditions that fear can be mobilized in, and how it can be used in favor of
conservative parties. The concept of "moral panic" (Cohen, 1972), coined in the
field of cultural studies, serves to illuminate the processes of conservative partisan mobilization. In my explanation, moral panic is a way of perceiving one's
political adversary as a threat that leads to mobilization based on reactionary fear.
Specifically, moral panic is expressed in the form of fear that a political movement, if it gains power, will destroy the social values defended by certain groups.
As has been shown in Nicola Beisel's work (1990), the actual power of the threat-
identified contender shapes the strength of the reaction movements. In cases of
powerful progressive movements (governments, parties in electoral ascendancy,
cultural movements with the capacity to influence lawmaking) that persist over
time, fear takes root in the sectors that see their interests threatened. The use of
threat as a moral appeal generates a sense of urgency and cohesion in the party's
social core behind a viable way out of that threat. While programmatic moderation brings new voters closer to the party, threat mobilization consolidates
hardcore support. In a democratic context of political polarization and tensions
associated with redistributive policies and cultural changes, the PRO's political
leaders activated a process of "moral panic" around redistribution and threats to

private property (Durand & Silva, 1998). The partisan "moral entrepreneurs" (Becker, 1963) took care to convince their audiences that a process of political radicalization would lead their country to "become Venezuela." They did so persistently and systematically, in electoral periods and at times of conflict. Indeed, to be effective, this mobilization has to be persistent over time and become part of the party's public image – as "the one that opposes ...," or "the one that protects us from ... ." The activation of moral panic is a coordinated activity by party builders and not just the result of isolated speeches by some leaders. Likewise, this moral appeal represents a valuable resource for new parties that need to build an "epic" that contributes to their internal cohesion and vitality (Rosenblatt, 2018).

The development of the PRO's organizational and ideational resources is based on two party mechanisms: on the one hand, the establishment of a homogeneous and centralized ruling coalition (Panebianco, 1988) that preserves the party brand (Lupu, 2016), and on the other, party boundaries that protect that brand over time from possible alterations, especially in the process of the party's territorial expansion. The adverse context of the party's initiation and early development incentivized the PRO's leaders to fear being instrumentalized by traditional parties or else being used by local leaders without a party, who could take advantage of the nascent brand to further their political careers. The PRO's ruling coalition thus established rigid control mechanisms over the use of the party brand, as well as candidate selection and political strategy. Recrear, in contrast, failed to establish coordination mechanisms between the leader and his inner circle and the provincial conservative-party partners.

Moreover, party leaders established a partisan division of labor that distributes selective incentives (positions, places on the lists) among leaders of traditional parties who joined PRO and collective incentives (party identity) among core party members (right-wing politicians, businessmen, NGO cadres). This allowed them to incorporate new politicians from the core who were recruited by the close-to-the-party organizations and given government positions, while places on the lists could be assigned to traditional politicians, all without ceding control over the party leadership. The case of the PRO corroborates that parties can organize and incorporate new social bases without threatening the power of their ruling coalition.

2 The Challenges of Latin American Conservative Parties in Recent History: The Argentina Case

The context in which conservative parties are born and in which they develop shapes the resources they can utilize as they build. However, party success is also accounted for by how leaders utilize resources, the types of decisions they make, and the mechanisms they establish to reproduce those resources over time. In Sections 3–5, I will describe how the PRO managed to produce programmatic innovation, build organizational resources, and mobilize the threat of the "Venezuela model" as a moral appeal in order to mobilize support. In this section I describe the context of the PRO and Recrear's emergence in order to identify the ideational and organizational resources (Panebianco, 1988) available at the time of launching these new parties. National contexts are key to understanding how conservative parties and party leaders managed to meet the structural and the historical challenges that had traditionally been faced by conservative parties. The historical weakness or strength of right-wing parties in each country, both in organizational and electoral terms (Middlebrook, 2000), shapes the resources that a conservative party can inherit from its predecessors. Meanwhile, the programmatic traditions available configure a favorable or unfavorable structure of opportunities for renewal. The period analyzed here is composed of the years since the "third wave" of democratization (Huntington, 1991) through the emergence and formation of the new parties. A study of a party's formative years allows us to understand how the PRO resolved, with the resources it had available, both its organizational challenges (Panebianco, 1988), and those related to its programmatic proposal. It will also allow us to identify the conditions under which Recrear's leaders, unlike their PRO competitors, failed to successfully address these challenges. Likewise, when parties are conceived of in a subnational district and begin to expand outward, as in the case of the PRO, it is also relevant to describe the subnational context of that emergence.

In this section, I first discuss the recent history of conservative parties in Argentina. I show that the PRO and Recrear had to address—in organizational and electoral terms—the historical weakness of conservative parties in that country (Di Tella, 1972; Gibson, 1996). This weakness implied, first, that their social and electoral bases were small and, second, that the parties that had preceded the PRO and Recrear were organizationally weak and therefore did not maintain an ongoing relevance in this field. At the same time, and to the new parties' benefit, pre-existing alternative right-wing parties were in crisis when the PRO and Recrear formed; those cadres were willing to look for new organizational options that could solve that crisis.

Next, I analyze the opening of a structure of political opportunities (Kitschelt, 1986) favorable to the formation of new parties: the severe crisis that began in Argentina in December 2001. This juncture created opportunities for new parties by making different types of resources available. The 2001–2 crisis had produced a crisis of party representativeness that affected non-Peronist groups in particular (Torre, 2003), among which were the small conservative parties and the UCR. This implied that both voters and political leaders abandoned their former ties and could be appealed to by a new party. This crisis was particularly intense in the city of Buenos Aires (Bril Mascarenhas, 2007), where the PRO began its party building.

The subnational path allowed the PRO to start the arid process of party building in a district with weak competitors and where traditional parties were in crisis. The decision to build a competitive party at the local level as a platform on which to build a national party was made by Macri and his close circle, and stood in contrast to the past decisions of some of his partners, as well as other conservative groups created in the same context, such as Recrear. This bet paid off when Macri acceded to the government of the city of Buenos Aires in 2007, which gave the PRO access to valuable public resources for party building: positions to distribute among leaders and activists, campaign financing, and clientelist and pork-barrel resources to distribute among its bases. With these resources, the PRO established an ideational and organizational basis for its nationalization, but also built a subnational stronghold. Strongholds are important because they allow for the cultivation of roots in order to recruit activists and build organizational resources, which should allow for survival over time (Tavits, 2013; Van Dyck, 2014). Parties must be able to overcome circumstantial electoral defeats. Thus, subnational strongholds serve to build party foundations (Cyr, 2017).

2.1 The Difficult Construction of a Successful Conservative Party in Argentina

Conservative parties have traditionally been weak in Argentina (Di Tella, 1972; Gibson, 1996).[8] This fact is among the factors that explain, for some authors, democratic instability during the twentieth century (Di Tella, 1972).[9] However, conservative ideas have still been influential. On the one hand, the majority parties included right-wing factions that had an important influence in some areas of public policy. On the other hand, despite the Argentine Right's limited electoral power relative to that of the majority parties, the Argentine Right

---

[8] As Kevin Middlebrook notes, "One of the principal legacies of nineteenth-century Argentine history was the absence of a nationally organized conservative party capable of contesting free elections under conditions of mass suffrage. By 1930, Argentine elites had turned to the armed forces as the most reliable defenders of their interests" (Middlebrook, 2000: 19).

[9] This electoral weakness on the part of the Right coincided with a weak capacity for the coordination of business groups, which privileged those groups' direct relationship with the state (lobbying, capture of privileged areas of accumulation, participation in government coalitions with reformist objectives) rather than the establishment of centralized organizations with the capacity for interest aggregation and collective action (Schneider, 2004).

managed to influence political power throughout the twentieth century through nonpartisan means, mainly the appointment of cadres in military governments (Morresi, 2015).

In 1983, when the nonelectoral pathway was closed, it was expected that a conservative party would emerge seeking to organize the political elites linked to that set of ideas, as well as the related electorate (Gibson, 1996). However, until 2007, the political right wing was dispersed and unstable. It was dispersed because only in a few cases were all the forces identified with liberal-conservative traditions unified.[10] It was unstable because even the most successful of these forces ended up disappearing or occupying a marginal place in the electoral competition. Attempts to build conservative forces were defused by the fact that the conservative leaders usually searched for shortcuts to power either through an agreement with traditional parties or by building electoral vehicles that followed the ups and downs of their leaders' popularity. The crisis or dissolution of conservative-party brands at the national level undoubtedly caused a coordination problem for political elites (Luna et al., 2021), who abandoned party life or had to rebuild their careers in other settings, but it also caused the defection of the conservative electorate (Lupu, 2016).[11]

The most relevant case of party decline due to the search for shortcuts to power through alliances with traditional parties was that of the Unión del Centro Democrático (Union of the Democratic Center, UCeDe), created in 1983 around an experienced neoliberal leader, Álvaro Alsogaray (Gibson, 1996). His programmatic proposal included a doctrinal and orthodox position on economic issues (a strong antistate orientation). In the 1983 presidential elections, UCeDe was the only national conservative party that obtained seats in Congress. In the 1987 mid-term elections, it was already a third national force, and in some districts, such as in the city of Buenos Aires, it obtained a sizeable percentage (18 percent) of the votes cast. In 1989, Alsogaray managed to unify liberal factions and many conservatives to form the Center Alliance (Table 1), which

---

[10] Unlike other Latin American cases, in Argentina there was no sharp separation between liberals and conservatives, either in ideological or partisan terms. This is due in part to the fact that, after the emancipation from Spain, the religious question did not occupy a relevant place in Argentina in the conflict among the elites. The term "liberal-conservative" applies to the political family associated with the political order founded in 1880 and with the political and intellectual Rights that, after the crisis of that order at the beginning of the twentieth century, kept that order as a reference. Thereafter, conservative political parties consolidated relatively successfully in the provincial arenas but were less successful at the national level. See in this regard Tato (2013).

[11] At the provincial level there were some provincial conservative parties with relative success (such as the Partido Demócrata – Democratic Party of Mendoza), as well as parties led by those security forces personnel that were closest to the authoritarian Right (Fuerza Republicana – Republican Force- in Tucumán, the Movimiento por la Dignidad y la Independencia – Movement for Dignity and Independence, MODIN – in the province of Buenos Aires). However, none of these forces succeeded in expanding to the national level.

obtained 9.8 percent of the votes in elections for the National Congress. However, it ended up dissolving in Peronism after the arrival of Carlos Menem to power in 1989. Menem's neoliberalism by surprise (Stokes, 2001) provided the UCeDe leaders with a shortcut to achieve power without winning elections. Many of the party leaders took positions in Menem's government and participated in electoral alliances with Peronism in its neoliberal version. Paradoxically, this shortcut eventually weakened the party organization to the extent that it nearly disappeared.

The most relevant case of a personalistic vehicle that followed the ups and downs of its leader's popularity was Acción por la República (Action for the Republic, AR), created by Domingo Cavallo in 1997. Cavallo was Minister of Economy in Menem's administration between 1991 and 1996 and achieved public renown for the success of his currency stabilization program. He left the Peronist government under allegations of official corruption, and shortly after he founded his own group with cadres that came from the liberal and conservative parties (Morresi & Vommaro 2014). In 1999, with AR allied with fragments of the provincial conservative parties, a conservative party was again a third national force in Argentine politics (Table 1). The following year, in the city of Buenos Aires, Cavallo came close to reaching the second round of elections to run against the candidate of an alliance between the UCR and the Front for a Country in Solidarity (Frepaso), a left-of-center party that was born as a split from Peronism at the beginning of Menem's administration. However, shortly afterwards, Cavallo agreed to return to be Minister of Economy, this time in the Alliance administration at the national level, and he shared the blame for the social and economic debacle that would end in the fall of that government in December 2001. Cavallo's loss of popularity caused the dissolution of the AR, just over four years after its creation. When the greatest economic and political crisis experienced by Argentina since the third wave of democratization began, there were no national conservative groupings left, the provincial parties were dispersed, and the leaders of the failed national parties were available, as were their constituencies.

2.2 The 2001–2 Crisis as a Favorable Context for the Creation of New Political Parties

The 2001 and 2002 crisis provided an opportunity for the emergence of new political forces. This is consistent with Levitsky, Loxton, and Van Dyck's (2016) suggestion regarding the role of conflict situations, as well as of shared traumas in creating the founding epic of a party (Rosenblatt, 2018). In Argentina, the rejection of traditional parties and the "political class" had been more intense

Table 1 The main center-right parties in Argentina and their electoral performance (1983–2015)

	1983	1989	1995	1999	2003	2007	2011	2015 and 2019
Main label	Federal Party in Federal Alliance	UCeDe in Center Alliance	UCeDe	Acción por la República	Recrear in Alliance Federal Movement to Recreate Growth	Recrear para el Crecimiento; Partido Popular de la Reconstrucción	No offer	PRO in Cambiemos (2015), then Juntos por el Cambio (2019) Alliance (with UCR, CC and others)
Programmatic features	Conservative Close relationship to military governments	Liberal-Conservative Rupture with militarism	Liberal-Conservative	Personalistic – neoliberal party. Anticorruption speech	Liberal-Conservative Orthodox and Republican economic discourse	Liberal-Conservative	Liberal-Conservative	Combination of neoliberalism, republican discourse and cultural pluralism
Total electoral performance*	2.2 percent	10.3 percent	2.2 percent	10.2 percent	16.7 percent	1.7 percent	-	34.1 percent (2015) 41.4 percent (2019)

* Aggregate scores obtained in presidential elections (first round) by the following forces;
1983: Liberal Autonomist Pact; Pampeano Federalist Movement; Federal Alliance; Socialist Democratic Alliance; National Confederation Center Alliance.
1989: Center Alliance; White of the Retired; Republican Force; Chaqueña action; Liberal Autonomist Pact-Progressive Democrat-Popular Liberation Movement; Democratic Party; Blue, Loyalty, Restoration; Of the Independence.
1995: Movement for Dignity and Independence; Alliance Front for Patriotic Coincidence; Republican Force.
1999: Alliance Action for the Republic.
2003: Federal Movement Alliance to Recreate Growth; Reconstruction Party; Movement for Dignity and Independence.
2007: Recrear for Growth; Popular Reconstruction Party.
2015: Alliance Let's Change/Cambiemos (first round).
2019: Together for Change/Juntos por el Cambio (first round).
Source: Author's own elaboration. Electoral data taken from the National Electoral Office.

among non-Peronist voters (Torre, 2003) and was particularly destructive of the party system in districts such as the city of Buenos Aires (Bril Mascarenhas, 2007). Conservative political actors saw the social and economic collapse of Argentina as a new opportunity to build their own party which, this time, would be autonomous from the discredited traditional leaders (Vommaro, Morresi, & Bellotti, 2015). The feeling of anomie and abrupt social decline caused by traditional political elites was the first "trauma" (Rosenblatt, 2018) to forge an identity among the political leaders who would create new partisan vehicles. At the same time, the recent history of conservative parties in the country posed two challenges. First, they needed to grow their electoral support in order not to be confined to being a third force with little chance of competing with traditional parties. Second, and relatedly, they needed to overcome the public skepticism of the neoliberal ideas that were seen as having caused the crisis of 2001 and 2002, and they needed to propose an economic program that would appeal to a broader electorate than just those on the Right.

In that context, two political formations emerged. One, called Recrear, was a clearly non-Peronist party, led by an orthodox economist, Ricardo López Murphy, and had a strong programmatic character. It maintained the canons of the dominant neoliberal economic discourse of the 1990s. This party managed to attract most of the provincial conservative parties and soon became a force that was national in scope (Vommaro, 2017). However, by 2007 it was showing signs of stagnation in electoral terms, as well as internal challenges to the leadership of López Murphy. The other party was the PRO. A few months before the collapse of Alianza government, a group of political leaders, elite NGOs activists, and businesspeople began to meet at the Creer y Crecer (To Believe and to Grow) Foundation in order to design political and policy projects. The Foundation had been created by Francisco de Narváez, a Peronist entrepreneur who had ventured into politics, but was headed by businessman Mauricio Macri. Macri is the heir to one of the largest Argentine fortunes (his father was the head of the Macri Societies Corporation [Sociedad Macri/ SOCMA] holdings, an economic group that had grown exponentially in the 1970s and 1980s, mainly due to state contracts) and, in 2001, he was president of Boca Juniors (the most popular soccer team in Argentina). Macri had shown an interest in entering into politics in the mid-1990s, but had delayed this decision until 2002. At that point, Macri and his inner circle decided that the time was right to build a new party. From the outset, it was viewed as a vehicle to achieve political power; the party's leaders chose to start at the local level in the city of Buenos Aires and build a nationally competitive party from there. The political alliance that linked Macri to De Narváez – who was looking to form a vehicle to compete at the national level – was dissolved.

The new party incorporated leaders from different backgrounds, who can be organized into five groups (Morresi & Vommaro, 2014): the first three groups were formed by long-standing politicians from the Peronist party, UCR, and conservative forces.[12] Conservative-party leaders were linked to federalist groups – such as the Partido Demócrata de la Capital Federal (Democratic Party of the Federal Capital) – that joined the PRO party early, as well as former UCeDe leaders (Arriondo, 2015) and the most recently formed conservative parties (the AR and Recrear). They came to the PRO convinced of the importance of building an electorally competitive party, for which they were willing to sacrifice, in most cases, ideological purity. Those who came from the UCR joined the PRO as part of an agreement between mid-level UCR leaders and Macri. They found in the PRO a space to advance their political careers, which had been blocked in the UCR, a party that was in crisis and was dominated by leaders from the 1980s (Persello, 2007). As for the Peronists, they were mostly mid-level leaders who came to PRO in its formative years (between 2002 and 2003, when it was still called Compromiso con el Cambio). Peronism in the city of Buenos Aires was in crisis at that time. These mid-level leaders found in the new party created by Macri and his group a competitive vehicle to access political positions.

The other groups comprised, firstly, new politicians drawn from NGOs and professional or international foundations, and, secondly, entrepreneurs and CEOs from the business world.[13] Businesspeople and NGO professionals and leaders were newcomers to political activity and although they shared some sociocultural features – for example, socio-occupational positions, worldviews, and a detachment from politics – they did not act concertedly as an intraparty group. Instead, they responded directly to the party leader's strategies and decisions. Businesspeople, at the beginning, were cadres of SOCMA, which had accompanied Macri during his time as president of Boca Juniors, and were integrated first into the Fundación Creer y Crecer and subsequently placed in positions associated with the management of finances in the government of the city of Buenos Aires.

After Recrear's poor results in the 2007 presidential elections and the arrival of the PRO to power in the city of Buenos Aires that same year,

---

[12] Individuals were classified by virtue of their last party membership prior to joining the PRO in the case of long-standing politicians. In the case of newcomers, their last occupation prior to joining the party was used as a criterion.

[13] These are not territorially based NGOs, but civil-society organizations associated with the upper-middle and upper classes, mostly connected to international funding networks. In Argentina, the main organizations of the urban poor have a territorial base and are connected with Peronism, with Trotskyist left-wing parties, or with the Catholic Church. The elite NGOs, although they have relations with territorial actors, are secondary actors in the world of the lower classes.

a group of Recrear leaders challenged López Murphy, imposed internal elections, and decided to merge with Macri's party (Vommaro, 2017), joining that partisan project as it was beginning to establish itself in a subnational stronghold and was seeking to be competitive at the national level. The PRO managed to unify the center-right and obtain national scope, although it was not yet competitive at the national level (Vommaro, 2017). Nonetheless, with the organizational resources of the richest subnational state in the country and a brand based on local management achievements, the PRO carried out a successful party-building process and became competitive in the national arena. In 2015, after erratic nationalization strategies, the PRO finally allied with the UCR, which gave it roots in districts where it had had weak support, and with other minor partners, including personalistic vehicles (Civic Coalition) and small niche parties. This strategy gave birth to the Cambiemos coalition, and in an environment of increasing rejection of center-left Kirchners' Peronism, which had been in government for twelve years, an electoral alliance led by a conservative party won the presidential elections for the first time in Argentina's history. Macri's government had a poor economic performance. It ended its time in power with higher levels of inflation, poverty, and unemployment than at the beginning. Likewise, it was unable to carry out the reformist agenda it had proposed after winning the mid-term elections in 2017 (Vommaro & Gené, 2022). In the 2019 presidential elections, Juntos por el Cambio, the new name of the PRO-led coalition, was defeated by the unified Peronism. This defeat triggered a process of leadership renewal in the PRO. Macri lost the place of undisputed leader that he had held since the beginning and challengers started a dispute for the party leadership. However, the party remained unified, managed to retain the government of the city of Buenos Aires, and achieved acceptable levels of coordination among its leaders in the 2021 mid-term elections, in which Juntos por el Cambio was again the list with the most votes. After two decades of party building, at the time of writing the PRO was preparing to lead a competitive coalition in the 2023 presidential elections.

At the time the PRO was founded, the heterogeneity of its membership, the mixed ideological positions of its cadres, and the strong leadership of Macri misled some observers, who had taken for granted that the newborn party was a sort of temporary vehicle for Macri's political entrance. Instead, the PRO managed to succeed. Indeed, Recrear, which had had better resources in the beginning, lost strength until it merged with the PRO. In the three following sections, I describe the factors that explain this outcome for the case of the PRO. Section 7 is devoted to explaining how these factors operate in the failed fate of Recrear.

3 The Programmatic Renewal of the Conservative Parties in Adverse Times

In this section I will show how the PRO managed to strengthen itself amidst the ascendancy of agendas associated with orientations traditionally contrary to the Right. In the terms of my model, I show that the party undertook a process of programmatic renewal that took a strikingly different path from the previous conservative political options that had provided the PRO with important ideational resources. This led to the construction of a powerful party brand, which gave solidity to the party in terms of adherence (Lupu, 2016). On the one hand, in the countries that had lived through dictatorships, as in Argentina, the Right had broken or deepened its rupture with that authoritarian past, turning down the possibility of obtaining organizational resources and moral cohesion for its party building (Loxton, 2016). This rupture had allowed it to bend to the democratic consensus of the "third wave" (Huntington, 1991) while avoiding proximity to actors accused of human rights violations, which constituted the "authoritarian baggage," that is, the negative ballast, of adherence to the dictatorships' legacy (Loxton, 2016). The PRO inherited that rupture, which had been made by the UCeDe in the 1980s (Gibson, 1996). When the defense of human rights became a topic of broad social consensus, the PRO did not have to defend marginal positions in the public debate. For a non-ASP conservative party, the absence of authoritarian baggage is an advantage, especially in contexts of broad anti-authoritarian consensus.

In the socioeconomic dimension, conservative parties that arise in the democratization process can take advantage, to some extent, of the discrediting of an earlier growth model that had involved a high level of state participation in the economy. This allows them to give a "reform and renovation" speech (Gibson, 1992: 35). This is the case of the UCeDe in Argentina, whose programmatic core resided in a doctrinal defense of economic (neo)liberalism and a firm criticism of state intervention in economic life. However, the ideological climate changed in the context of the "pink tide" that brought left-leaning governments to power in much of early twenty-first-century Latin America. In that context, the conservative parties must deal with a consensus in many of the countries in favor of state intervention in the economy (Levitsky & Roberts, 2011; Luna & Rovira Kaltwasser, 2014). To be competitive, PRO leaders chose to moderate both their pro-market economic public positions and their public positions on cultural issues (Morresi & Vommaro, 2014).

Another phenomenon of programmatic innovation is the search for new issues either not taken up or abandoned by the party's main competitors, such as specific problem-solving capacity (the government as "management") and security. Privileging general problem-solving capacity was a way for the PRO to avoid strong doctrinal positions. Through local management, it built a positive attribute—"getting things done"—for its party brand (Morresi & Vommaro, 2014). Meanwhile, some PRO leaders used security matters to connect with lower-class constituencies (Morresi & Vommaro, 2014).

In order to carry out this work, the party had an organizational mechanism that proved to be efficient. This was the existence of a centralized ruling coalition (Panebianco, 1988), which controlled from the party's beginnings not only the party program, but also its the electoral strategy and, from 2007 onward, government communications. This ruling coalition was formed by Macri and his inner circle, joined by some political newcomers (businessmen and professionals from elite NGOs) and a handful of leaders from the conservative parties. It was stable over time and achieved levels of coordination in the party's discourse and between government action, program, and electoral strategy.

3.1 Exit the Electoral Niche: The Programmatic Challenges of the PRO Party

Argentine conservative parties had historically had a strongly doctrinal character, and had concentrated their program on economic issues (Morresi, 2015). With these characteristics they remained minority electoral options, even in the case of the successful UCeDe in the 1980s (Gibson, 1996). The challenge for the PRO was to build a discourse capable of reaching wider constituencies. For this, it focused on two issues: first, on its character as a new party (Vommaro & Morresi, 2014) that would solve the problems that the traditional political class had not been able to solve; second, on a platform based on management and efficiency, that is, on a nonideological approach to solving the specific problems citizens faced, especially related to urban infrastructure issues (transportation, sanitation, care of green spaces) (Vommaro, Morresi, & Bellotti, 2015). These attributes became the core of the PRO party brand (Lupu, 2016). Also, both of the above programmatic strategies show that the PRO was built as a party that sought to compete for power rather than to become a platform for the propagation of ideas (Vommaro & Morresi, 2014).

The PRO's novelty was consistent with the incorporation of new cadres from the business and NGO worlds. In the city of Buenos Aires, the party comprised similar proportions of old and new politicians: According to my 2011 survey, 54 percent came from the Peronist, Radicalist, or right-wing parties, while 46 percent had recently entered politics from the business or NGO worlds (2011 survey). However, party leaders always chose to present themselves as "newcomers," which was a positive attribute given the loss of public confidence in established politicians in the wake of the 2001–2 crisis, which had taken place during the PRO's foundational phase.

The PRO's presentation of itself as a pro-market party focused on "efficiency" and "management" rather than ideology was compatible with the strategy of starting at the local government level and from there, building a nationally competitive electoral option. Local politics is a propitious space for political platforms based on the technical resolution of specific problems (Landau, 2018). Also, in solving concrete problems, the PRO incorporated elements of political traditions outside the Argentinean center-right, such as the promotion of ecology – associated especially with waste recycling – and cultural public policies linked to progressivism. Moreover, by being anchored at the local level, the PRO built a discourse on security that, without directly embracing the idea of the *mano dura*, made the fight against crime one of its main public-policy axes.

3.2 A Programmatic Renewal in Three Steps

The program-building process consisted of three fundamental steps, determined not only by the change in party label, but also by the incorporation of new political groups and by the redefinition of strategic identity elements based on political conjunctures and the needs of party building (see Table 2).

The program-building process began in 2002–3 with the adoption of the Compromiso para el Cambio (Commitment to Change) label. The central components of the party's platform revolved around the importation of values from the private sector into the public sector – "efficient management" – and the greater transparency of a "new politics," contrasted against traditional methods. The style was technocratic. As Macri was president of the Boca Juniors football club, he also gave a nod to popular culture, although while maintaining a conservative tenor (Ostiguy, 2009). In 2005, the PRO made a brand change in the context of an alliance between Macri's group and Recrear. The name Propuesta Republicana (Republican Proposal) and the acronym PRO were devised to convey the idea of a modern force (being PRO meant both "trendy" and "of good quality"). A communication team led by PRO collaborators – who would later continue to be part of the communication teams of that party – designed the new image. The relationship with Recrear's partners was tense and poorly coordinated. In fact, in the 2005 elections, the only one in which the two groups competed as allies, the PRO focused on winning in the city of Buenos Aires, where it consolidated an electoral strategy centered on local management issues (Calvo, 2005), while Recrear maintained a harsh discourse of opposition

Table 2 The labels of the new center-right in Argentina (2002–15)

	2002–2003	2005	2015/2019
Label			
Political groups	Compromiso para el Cambio Entrepreneurs, NGO leaders, and traditional right-wing politicians (founding group) + Radicals (UCR members) and Peronists who left their parties	Propuesta Republicana (PRO) Alliance with Recrear para el Crecimiento, incorporation of provincial right-wing parties	Cambiemos/Juntos por el Cambio Alliance with UCR, the Coalición Cívica and other minor parties
Programmatic Components	Management and expert knowledge. Defense of the "new politics"	Solving specific problems (transportation, sanitation, green spaces), break with ideological definitions, adoption of postmaterial values (ecology), and an emphasis on security	Centrality of antipopulism and the transparency agenda

Source: Author's own work.

to the FPV national government based on the criticism of the deficit in public budgets and the concentration of power in the Executive Branch. The PRO complemented the managerial discourse with the adoption of postmaterial values like environment protection. It also adopted a tone anchored in emotions rather than in political rationales.[14] For Macri and his inner circle, the hypothesis was that this tone would allow them to further transcend the ideological core of the center-right. After the 2005 elections, Macri's and López Murphy's groups separated and the PRO label and the attributes built around it remained in Macri's hands.

The PRO label and the discursive turn around solving concrete problems with an emotional tone was maintained in the 2007 elections in the city of Buenos Aires, which gave the PRO access to a subnational government for the first time. The government of the city of Buenos Aires would work to finish establishing the components that defined the PRO brand from then on. "Doing" (efficiency) and innovation became central elements of the party's visual aesthetics and the party platform (Figures 1 and 2). Pro-market ideas were framed in terms of the values of efficiency and innovation. Meanwhile, the adoption of the label Cambiemos (Let's Change) in 2015 – a product of the electoral coalition with the UCR, the Civic Coalition, and other minor allies, which favored the dominant position of the PRO in the non-Peronist space – gave the PRO access to the center electorate and, at the same time, to the mobilization of the transparency agenda linked to that constituency.

Figure 1 "Doing Buenos Aires," government advertising, 2007

---

[14] The PRO did not write an official party manifesto until 2015, at the insistence of its Radical partners in the Cambiemos coalition. One of the previous attempts to define a program was made by the party's communication and discourse team. In 2009, this team drafted the document "Our idea," which defined the party's identity based on three dimensions: "closeness (empathy)," "positivity," and "the future." The document was written in the style of self-help books and avoided making ideological references (cf. Vommaro, 2015).

Figure 2 "We achieved in two years more than others did in ten years. We are recovering lost time," campaign poster, 2009

Figure 3 "Doing what needs to be done," government advertising, 2016

Brand development remained anchored in the two original components: the party of the new cadres that "got into politics," and "management" as a program of action based on concrete problem-solving, that is to say, going beyond ideology. Likewise, the Cambiemos coalition framed its national government action in terms of a narrative of "doing" (Figure 3).

Throughout the process, the intraparty ruling coalition led by Macri maintained tight control of brand development. Having learned the lessons of the recent history of conservative forces in Argentina that had been absorbed by traditional parties, or had experienced crises when allied with those forces, PRO leaders set out from the beginning to build an autonomous political strategy. Macri's leadership managed to overcome internal challenges during the foundational stage of the party – when the PRO lists were used by some free-rider politicians as a platform to win a parliamentary seat (Morresi & Vommaro, 2014) – and to impose himself, later, as *primus inter pares* among the leaders of the allied parties. Besides, Macri and his inner circle established a ruling coalition capable of controlling the party label and the party brand (and a certain identity associated with it) and of selecting candidates compatible with that brand both at the national and, in many cases, also at the subnational level, in order to offer the electorate personalities whose public image was consistent with the party program. Provincial leaders mentioned in interviews that the ruling coalition established in the city of Buenos Aires delivered at election time a "turnkey" kit with everything needed to carry out the campaign: prepared speeches, posters, and flyers, as well as proselytism manuals for leaders and activists, with "campaign axes" and prepared phrases.[15] This ruling coalition, comprising new politicians from the elite NGO and business worlds as well as leaders of the traditional Right, prevented the party from being colonized by free-riders or by other political forces, but also provided a systematic and coordinated discursive framework for leaders coming from different political traditions, even those that were opposed to conservative groups, such as politicians from traditional parties (Peronism and the UCR).

Indeed, according to the 2011 survey I conducted, PRO leaders with different backgrounds not only have uneven political experiences, but also differences in regards to ideological self-positioning and their opinions on central issues in Argentine political life. The intraparty group most dissonant from the average of PRO leaders' opinions is that with a UCR background. According to our data, the PRO leaders with UCR backgrounds have, on average, an ideological self-positioning more to the left than the other intraparty groups and are consistent with less conservative positions than the average of all PRO leaders, both on economic and cultural issues. On distributive issues, former Radicals (UCR members), on average, express lower levels of agreement with the idea that the market is the best allocator of resources, and greater agreement with the idea that the privatization of public services carried out in the 1990s, during the Menem administration, was a failed policy. The position regarding the public or private nature of these services is a good indicator of ideological positioning. The discrediting of Menemist Peronism as a political movement was uneven among PRO leaders. The work of the leading unification and coordination

---

[15] We consulted some of these manuals, as in the case of the province of Córdoba.

coalition at the programmatic level was crucial to achieving coherence in this area. The positions of the PRO leaders with Radical origins are also, on average, more progressive in the cultural field (support for the consideration of a law to legalize abortion) and in the social field (less support for the *mano dura* on security matters and for harsh laws that restrict the arrival of immigrants). Meanwhile, while leaders coming from Peronism have smaller differences in ideological self-positioning with leaders from backgrounds associated with conservative groups (business elites and leaders with a past in conservative parties) than former Radicals, as well as having fewer differences with the party's average positions on economic issues, they differ in their views on central political issues. Leaders with a Peronist background have, on average, more positive positions on the role of unions in Argentine politics. That is, they are more likely to believe in the power of the formal lower classes to exercise a veto in the public-policy arena. They also are less likely to emphatically defend a procedural conception of democracy associated with the separation of powers, which progressively began to form part of the programmatic nucleus of the PRO, associated with the "republican" position.

The ruling coalition's control over the program became crucial not only because of the heterogeneity of the PRO cadres in term of backgrounds, but also because it permitted them to moderate and model their pro-market positions, which are part of the ideological core of conservative ideas and are compatible with the party's social core. Indeed, PRO leaders who are economic elites as well as former conservative leaders have an ideological self-positioning clearly more to the right than those of leaders with other backgrounds and, consistently, tend to be closer to traditional conservative positions in all the economic, cultural, and social issues. Those leaders defended some of the fundamental values of neo-liberalism in Argentina: the value of the market as the best and most effective mechanism for allocating resources and the independence of the Central Bank with respect to the Executive Branch in setting monetary policy. They also disagreed with the idea that the privatization of public services carried out in the 1990s, during the Menem administration, had been a failure of that period. On political issues, the positions of PRO leaders coming from economic elites and conservative parties but also from NGOs – which have an ideological self-positioning that is more to the left than the previous two – are also conservative, and follow the tradition of the Argentine Right. For example, they oppose the power of unions in politics and they support the adoption of stricter measures to regulate the arrival of migrants in the country. In the field of human rights, a subject closely associated with the progressive tradition in Argentina and strongly mobilized as an emblem during the cycle of the Peronist FPV, PRO leaders except those coming from the UCR and the NGOs consider that "the most important thing is to look forward and not backward." "Looking forward" refers to abandoning the emphasis on prosecuting those responsible for crimes against humanity committed during the last military dictatorship.

Together with these conservative features, the majority of PRO leaders incorporate heterodox elements regarding the conservative tradition, especially a favorable view of state intervention to reduce income differences. This positioning gives an account, first, of the incorporation of statist elements that moderate the pro-market program; and, second, of the majority consensus in favor of certain cash-transfer programs for the lower classes that have been implemented since the 2000s in the context of the "pink tide" (Garay, 2016). The PRO had to accept some of the public goods introduced during the center-left cycle in the field of social policy (Niedzwiecki & Pribble, 2018).

The tension between the cadres' ideas and their ability to defend those ideas in public as well as their ability to implement those ideas once in office is typical of any competitive party. Thus, although the PRO built a "purpose" (Rosenblatt, 2018) around a pro-market program, the PRO's public appeals privileged electoral competitiveness over its programmatic goals. The attributes of the party brand were administered by the ruling coalition, which vetoed the ideas of some of its leaders and even removed officials from their positions when they manifested conservative ideas in public, especially in the fields of culture and education. This was more important at the beginning of their government of the city of Buenos Aires, when the PRO brand was under construction. For example, Macri decided not to appoint a Minister of Culture who "despised conceptual art and [the] avant-garde."[16] Some time later, a writer had to resign twelve days after being appointed Minister of Education for espousing authoritarian positions in the media, using the language of the Cold War to refer to his adversaries.[17] The PRO's leading coalition also worked internally on moderating the discourse of party leaders and activists. In my fieldwork I witnessed meetings with activists in which one of the members of the leading coalition, founder of the youth branch of the party, would ask those present to avoid references to past political figures or even to avoid defining political ideology in their proselytizing activities. For example, when a student from the Universidad Católica Argentina asked whether party activists could at least vindicate the liberalism of the nineteenth century, the PRO leader answered "they are not categories that represent us. We are a twenty-first century party."[18]

---

[16] "Macri consideró que Luis Rodríguez Felder no era 'PRO,'" *Perfil*, October 25, 2007.

[17] "Renunció Posse: duró apenas 11 días como ministro de Educación porteño," *Perfil*, December 23, 2009.

[18] Ethnographic observation by the author, Jóvenes PRO meeting, July 2014.

On the contrary, in security matters, the PRO assumed a discourse that was more aligned with the conservative positions of its leaders. The issue of security is one of the most persistent topics on the public agenda in Argentina (Kessler, 2009) and conservative forces have always found it favorable ground for their programmatic appeals, even more so when faced with the hesitations of progressivism on the matter. In this vein, Macri and his collaborators took advantage of this unaddressed issue to position themselves as spokespersons of a security discourse based on expressing empathy with the victims of crime and amplifying a broader social concern. To this end, since the local election campaign of 2007, Macri started a campaign in favor of the creation of a local police force – until then the policing of the district had been in the charge of the Federal Police.

One of the biggest programmatic challenges for the PRO lay in the consensus that had been gained by the progressive cultural agenda on gender and sexual and reproductive rights, particularly in the city of Buenos Aires. Macri and his inner circle moved away from the conservative positions traditionally predominant in the Argentine right wing and gave voice to party leaders promoting progressive positions on these issues. In addition, Macri always showed himself to be distant from the Catholic Church and even publicly promoted his meditation practice and his approach to Buddhism (Vommaro, Morresi, & Bellotti, 2015). In terms of public policy, as head of government of the city of Buenos Aires, Macri declared himself in favor of gay marriage in 2009, before Congress passed a national law legalizing it. Indeed, when a judge enabled two men to marry, Macri rejected an appeal to the decision and even publicly hailed the future marriage: "The world is going in this direction. We have to live together and accept this reality. I wish them happiness".[19] Moreover, during his presidency, Macri enabled congressional debate of a law that proposed the legalization of abortion. In all cases, the party maintained a balanced position; it did not fail to shelter conservative leaders or maintain ties with the Catholic and evangelical churches. The abortion law was not approved in 2018, in good part because neither Macri nor most of his party leaders supported it. In any case, the result of this two-front strategy was that PRO stopped positioning itself in line with traditional right-wing conservatism.

After 2008, and even more since 2011, when political polarization intensified in Argentina, PRO increasingly promoted an anti-Kirchner discourse. This is consistent with its electoral core's behavior. On the one hand, the middle and upper-middle classes mobilized massively in 2008 in the context of the conflict between the Cristina Fernández de Kirchner administration and the agricultural

---

[19] *Clarín*, November 14, 2009 (www.clarin.com/ediciones-anteriores/macri-dio-fuerte-respaldo-matrimonio-homosexuales_0_HJNgYfdC6Kx.html).

producers over export taxes after the government of Kirchner proposed an increase in these taxes in response to the increase in the international price of grain (Mangonnet, Murillo, & Rubio, 2018). They mobilized again, in 2012 and 2013 in *cacerolazos* (a protest consisting of banging pots and pans common among the middle classes in Argentina and Latin America) that had both economic (unregulated access to dollars) and institutional (against corruption and threats to independent justice) demands (Gold & Peña, 2019). On the other hand, as we will see in Section 4, a "moral panic" was disseminated among the PRO's social core, linked to the possibility of "chavization" in Argentina (Vommaro, 2017); that is, a drift away from capitalism and democracy. In these years, a forceful reaction to Kirchnerist populism was organized and politically framed by the PRO in the 2015 presidential elections. However, in his programmatic proposal, the presidential candidate Macri emphasized his acceptance of some policies initiated during the "pink tide" that had generated a broad consensus, such as the quasi-universal cash-transfer program Asignación Universal por Hijo (Universal Child Allowance), which had been implemented in the context of the 2009 international crisis during the government of Cristina Fernández de Kirchner and covered any unemployed or underemployed person earning less than the minimum monthly salary with children under eighteen years of age or who had a disability; or state ownership of certain companies, such as the national airline, which had been nationalized during the same Kirchnerist Peronist administration after poor private management.[20]

In sum, the PRO made a programmatic shift toward moderation in relation to the traditional right wing in socioeconomic and cultural matters. This allowed it to win a centrist electorate in a scenario of progressive distributive consensuses. In coordinating this strategy, centralized control of the brand and public discourse by Macri and the ruling coalition was crucial. At the same time, in order to gain relevance in the debate, the new party took advantage of vacant ground on a topic which progressive parties are traditionally more averse toward tackling, while conservative parties have more kinship with it – that of security, which was also seen by many as an entangled issue.

4 The Construction of New Organizational Mechanisms for Party Mobilization

Conservative parties have to face two types of challenges in terms of organizational resources. First, they had to establish lasting ties with their core

---

[20] Ideological moderation as a stage prior to a party's coming to power has been analyzed with regard to leftist forces in Latin America, especially in the case of the Workers' Party in Brazil (see Hunter, 2010).

constituency, and especially with economic elites. This was even more the case when these elites were indifferent to party ideology and cared mainly about whether the party in office – right-wing or not – would guarantee a good "business climate." The economic elites' support is both a source of financing and a source of support for government coalitions. The second challenge was to build linkages with wider constituencies than those traditionally close to the right. To solve the first challenge, PRO leaders built close-to-the-party organizations – NGOs, think tanks, and foundations – that allowed it to mobilize economic elites over time. These new organizational resources enabled the party to attract businessmen with dispersed loyalties. Think tanks, NGOs, and foundations recruited and mobilized businesspeople who were not politically active, channeled scattered support, helped with fundraising, and served as a programmatic source for the new party. Newcomer leaders coming from the business world created most of these close-to-the-party organizations and acted as mobilizers and organizers (Han, 2014) of activists in their upper-middle and upper-class social environments. In this section I will analyze the Generación 2025 Foundation (G25), through which the PRO managed to organizationally penetrate the world of entrepreneurs and CEOs, recruiting people as candidates for political office and for appointment to government positions (Vommaro, 2017). The G25 imitated the organizational format of exclusive business elite clubs such as the Young Presidents' Organization (YPO). In addition, the PRO, together with the think tank the Pensar Foundation, organized business-world actors to design government programs in their areas of expertise (Echt, 2020). These foundations are not always part of the formal party organization. The G25, in fact, is defined as "linked" to the PRO without being part of its organizational chart (Vommaro, 2017). However, all these informal mediations are part of the political parties' environment (Sawicki, 1997) and allow these parties to communicate with and organize economic elites, their core constituency. The concept of the "party environment" (Sawicki, 1997) focuses on the social environments – small organizations, informal groups, and so on – that extend a party's life beyond its formal organization. The concept refers to a porous zone between the organization and its environment in which formal and informal social spaces are part of the daily life of the parties, beyond their explicit purposes (Offerlé, 1987). For instance, in the case of Argentine Peronism Levitsky identified the basic units – territorial base committees – as the fundamental units of the party's grassroots, even if they had no place defined in the party's organizational chart. Other types of informal instance may include NGOs and foundations close to the parties, but also religious circles and union movements. Among these instances, some form what I call the parties' "social worlds of belonging" (Vommaro, 2017), since they are rooted in individuals' core social environment. In Latin America, leftist parties usually have this nucleus in the working classes (Levitsky & Roberts, 2011); meanwhile, conservative have their social worlds of belonging among the social and economic elites (Gibson, 1996).

The conservative parties also need to build organizational resources to connect with noncore constituencies. Such mediations have enabled the parties to expand the Right's electoral bases. The PRO incorporated former Peronist and UCR cadres that mobilized working- and middle-class electorates. In the populous southern part of the city of Buenos Aires, for example, Peronist leaders control PRO activity and connect that party with the area's inhabitants (Morresi & Vommaro, 2014). Likewise, leaders coming from Peronism and UCR provide links with social organizations associated with the lower classes that allow the PRO to gain a foothold in constituencies traditionally distanced from conservative parties. These leaders have access to the resources of the government of the city of Buenos Aires (jobs, public positions), with which they have been able to reward their most loyal brokers and activists, who favored the rooting of the new party in lower-class neighborhoods.

To amalgamate these heterogeneous fragments and ensure levels of coordination between ambitious political leaders with different backgrounds, the PRO ruling coalition established a partisan division of labor that allowed it to distribute selective incentives (Panebianco, 1988) among traditional politicians while maintaining control of the political and brand strategy in the hands of a small ruling coalition formed by newcomers and, to a lesser extent, by politicians from former conservative parties, such as UCeDe (Vommaro & Armesto, 2015).

The establishment of stable relations with this core constituency and the political mobilization of secondary constituencies was an organizational achievement on the part of the PRO that required decisions to be made by party leaders, as we will see in the following subsections.

4.1 Mobilizing and Organizing Uncoordinated Economic Elites

Investing in organization building was not the most obvious option for a party like the PRO, founded by an entrepreneur as a personalistic project. In fact, the first organizational format adopted by the Macri group and its inner circle was that of the think tank (Creer y Crecer). However, over time, the PRO's leaders managed to build organizational resources linking the party with its core constituency, which allowed it to mobilize activists, recruit new leaders and cadres to government positions, and obtain financial support. They achieved this by virtue of having carried out their main organizational strategy: the creation of close-to-the-party organizations adapted to social worlds related to the party – the business and NGO worlds – allowing the PRO to recruit cadres and import repertoires of action and aesthetics that were consistent with the party brand.

The organizational mediations adapted to its core constituency were think tanks and NGOs that functioned as informal organizations of a relationship with economic elites. This point was critical in a country where, as I pointed out, the upper classes had little party representation (Di Tella, 1972; Gibson, 1996) and the economic elites established particularistic and informal links with the political sphere, privileging direct relationships with the state (Schneider, 2004). In fact, economic elites had established good relations with Peronism in the 1990s, when the neoliberal turn took place under Carlos Menem. So it was necessary for PRO leaders who came from the business and NGO worlds to mobilize their colleagues, both with arguments regarding the importance of participating in politics, and with organizational structures that were hospitable to social groups that, after the 2001 –2 economic crisis, had lost their faith in the political parties but had greater incentives to "do something for the country."

These PRO leaders used foundations that functioned as "bridges" between the political and the business and NGO worlds. These close-to-the-party organizations are of two types: first, creations of the party or of its leaders, such as foundations and think tanks that incorporate entrepreneurs, CEOs, and upper-class activists; second, pre-existing institutions with which the PRO established fluid and permanent linkages, such as university student centers of private and denominational universities (Grandinetti, 2015) and NGOs working on social issues. Both types of organizations are part of the PRO "party environment" (Sawicki, 1997).

The foundations and think tanks created by the party or by some of its leaders installed subsidiaries throughout the country, recruited activists, and mobilized audiences from the economic elites. In districts where the party had a weak presence, these subsidiary organizations functioned as a replacement for party leaders. They functioned as points of contact, mobilization, and recruitment of people from the business and the NGO worlds who otherwise would not have engaged in traditional party activity. The Pensar Foundation is in charge of designing PRO government programs.[21] The G25 was founded in 2008 on the

---

[21] The Pensar Foundation arose from an initiative of intellectuals and center-right political leaders. They considered it necessary, at the end of the 2001–2 crisis, to create a think tank that would propagate conservative ideas, in the image of the Spanish Foundation for Social Analysis and Studies (FAES), created by Luis María Aznar in 1989. With the growth of PRO, and the entrance to that party of many of the Pensar members, the Foundation joined the party and in 2010 its objectives were redefined: It was to design government programs for the PRO national government project. See Echt (2020).

initiative of Esteban Bullrich and Guillermo Dietrich, two former managers. Its objective is to recruit businessmen and managers for the PRO administration (both at the subnational and national levels). The G25 is defined as "an autonomous and self-sufficient foundation with respect to the Party, identified with the PRO's values" (G25, 2014: 8). The G25 foundation staff spoke the same language as those who had come from the business world. Both foundations were "friendly" territories and at the same time provided tasks tailored to what businessmen could do to contribute to the political project. They used rituals and the logic of sociability taken from the social worlds with which they were linked. In fact, much of the G25's organizational format was imported from exclusive CEO clubs such as the YPO: the mentoring of newcomers and the organization of small containment groups to work on the affective impact of the passage to political activity (Vommaro, 2017). The PRO's leaders asked CEOs for commitments of varying intensity. They managed to articulate different ways of delivering time and/or money to promote the PRO brand, which, from the activists' point of view, turned their small and punctual acts (a Facebook post, the organization of a meeting with candidates in their homes) into a coordinated contribution (or a node in a network, to use the actors' terms). The organization G25 Mujeres (G25 Women) played a key role in these activities. Created in 2013, G25 Mujeres enables members of the managers' social environment to become activists. This branch of the organization allowed members of the upper and upper-middle classes to find a channel for political participation during the time when the Peronist mobilization was dominant. Han's (2014) studies on how civil organizations recruit activists showed that to be successful they must have mobilizers – persons capable of attracting people – and organizers, that is, those who take care of giving newcomers a place. These two tasks enable the organizational conversion of these newcomers into activists. That was the task of the PRO leaders who actively participated in these close-to-the-party organizations. The establishment of a wide range of activities, in terms of investment of time, resources, and career, accounts for the adaptation of these devices to audiences who were not always ready for a more complete conversion into activists or politicians.

The PRO's mobilization of managers and CEOs and their social environment was successful and had two effects: First, it produced the large volume of electoral activism that now forms the core of the PRO party. In 2012, the G25 had 800 adherents. By 2013, it had 2450 adherents, comprising a similar proportion of men and women (G25, 2013: 21). By 2014, the G25 had been able to establish a regional branch in thirteen of Argentina's twenty-four provinces. For its part, G25 Mujeres already had three established "territorial committees" – Capital, North Zone, and West Zone – and claimed to include more than 7,000 women in social networks. By 2008, the PRO had, at the national level, 35,676 adherents. So the volume of activism that G25 added was significant. Second, it produced a massive entry of managers and CEOs into the government: 31 percent of the occupants of senior positions in the Cambiemos government (initial cabinet) had had a senior management role in the private sector before 2015. Among the ministers, in 2017, 50 percent still held positions in private company directories.[22]

In summary, the PRO provided a variety of opportunities for participation in its core activism, from social media activism to participation in the design of government programs, in proselytizing activities and in electoral control. It combined a permanent—though in many cases a part-time—involvement with a seasonal activism, latent in social networks and particularly intense during electoral campaigns (Vommaro, 2017).

4.2 Incorporating Secondary Constituencies by Recruiting Available Leaders from Traditional Parties

While mediations with the business world were more accessible to Macri and his inner circle, the lower- and middle-class constituencies were socially distant from the traditional constituents of conservative parties in Argentina. This problem was solved through the incorporation of cadres from traditional parties capable of mobilizing voters from lower- and middle-class sectors. These leaders had access to Buenos Aires city government resources to reward loyal brokers and activists.

To establish the social anchors of the PRO leaders I used a question from my 2014–15 survey of a nonprobability sample of PRO leaders in the city of Buenos Aires that provided an indication of the interviewees' relationships with different associations. I recoded the answers lumping together previous and current participation in eight different types of associations. According to my data, the different leaders' backgrounds are related to different social anchors. This scheme allows us to infer that the PRO managed, through the incorporation of these heterogeneous cadres, to establish links with different constituencies. Leaders belonging to the PRO's social core provide links with organizations typical of this core. The newcomers (economic elites and members of elite NGOs) are more strongly linked than the other intraparty groups to professional associations (67.7 percent of newcomers versus 38 percent of leaders coming from traditional parties) and business chambers (33 percent of

---

[22] According to a study by the Elites Observatory (IDAES-UNSAM) that surveyed all the occupants of high positions in the initial cabinet of the Macri government and recorded, among other data, their last job before taking office.

newcomers versus 16.5 percent of leaders coming from traditional parties). Leaders with a background in conservative parties add the most links with exclusive-membership clubs (followed closely in this by leaders with a Peronist background). Leaders who started their career in the PRO and therefore have no previous relevant activity provide weak social roots, except with professional associations, probably because many of them are lawyers who are active in the conservative Colegio de Abogados de la Ciudad de Buenos Aires (City of Buenos Aires Bar Association).

Our data also show that leaders coming from the UCR and Peronist parties provide links with two types of organizations typical of lower-class, union, and territorial and community organizations, with which the other PRO leaders have weaker or nonexistent links. The PRO social core's aloof relationship with lower- and middle-class organizations is thus compensated for by the incorporation of Peronist and UCR leaders, who channel these connections: 50 percent of those with a Peronist background and 33.3 percent of those with a UCR background have or have had relations with trade unions, compared to 0 percent of newcomers. Besides, 87.5 percent of those with a Peronist background and 83.3 percent of those with a UCR background have or have had relations with community and territorial organizations, compared to 33.3 percent of newcomers. In effect, the former Peronist and UCR leaders were responsible for recruiting activists in the southern lower-class neighborhoods of the city of Buenos Aires and in middle-class neighborhoods (Vommaro, Morresi, & Bellotti, 2015). Maintaining these activists as participants and supporters depended on the party's access to patronage goods (jobs and public positions, as well as public contracts), by virtue of the party's control of, at first, the local government, and later, the national government (Vommaro & Armesto, 2015).

Beyond their diverse backgrounds, PRO leaders have a high rate of participation in close-to-the-party organizations, that is, NGOs and think tanks created by party leaders to mobilize and organize different constituencies. This suggests that the incorporation of leaders with heterogeneous backgrounds in the core party organizations favors intraparty cohesion and contributes to success.

The mediations provided by the leaders of the traditional parties were crucial in establishing linkages with secondary constituencies both in the city of Buenos Aires and in the rest of the country. In the city of Buenos Aires, from the outset the PRO achieved high voting rates in the poor southern districts by virtue of its alliance with Peronist leaders. These leaders held posts that gave them access to important patronage resources. For example, Peronist Cristian Ritondo, with long history of militancy in the lower-class southern zone of Buenos Aires, was, at first vice president of the legislature of the city of Buenos Aires between 2011 and 2015. In my fieldwork I interviewed Peronist brokers from lower-class neighborhoods in the southern zone who had a job in the legislature and had been hired by Ritondo. For example, in an interview with a broker from Villa 20, in Villa Soldati, five others who worked with that community leader also took part. All of them had jobs in the legislature. Electoral research shows how the party initially managed to attract poor voters. In the 2005 mid-term elections, the PRO was the main recipient of right-of-center votes (as the UCeDe had been in 1995), but it also took a significant proportion of the vote that in 1995 had gone to the Peronists, a territory beyond the reach of other conservative groups such as Recrear (Alessandro, 2009: 602–603). The incorporation of UCR leaders occurred later, because they were part of another electoral alliance until 2006. By 2007, however, the PRO had already incorporated Radical leaders from the center areas of the city of Buenos Aires. They also held positions with access to employment and other patronage resources. Although there is no evidence that patronage resources are directly profitable from an electoral point of view, they were important for PRO's party building, especially in consolidating a multiclass coalition.

The alliance with leaders of traditional parties, especially the Radical party, also played a crucial role in the nationalization of the PRO. If we take the PRO's participation in federal elections under its own label as an indicator of territorial establishment (Table 3), the alliance with Recrear and with provincial conservative parties that took place after 2007 enabled the PRO to increase its degree of nationalization, but left it still short of truly national coverage.[23] The incorporation of Peronist and Radical leaders occurred throughout the period, although with greater intensity after 2009 (when the PRO established an alliance with anti-Kirchner Peronists in some districts). This incorporation gave the party its maximum level of district presence, which decreased as a result of its decision not to participate in the 2011 presidential elections. The PRO then maintained the total number of districts in which it had a presence, but the number of provinces in which the acronym PRO was not visible increased, and in contrast, the number of provinces in which that party controlled the label decreased. In 2013, meanwhile, the two strategies for incorporating cadres – adding leaders of traditional parties and adding outsiders – gave new impetus to the national expansion of the party. But after more than ten years of life, the PRO still could not compete in all the country's districts, and only in seven districts did it compete under its own label.

Only from 2015 on, by means of the Cambiemos alliance, did the PRO manage to run candidates in all districts. Thus, the incorporation of politicians from traditional parties, as well as an alliance with one of them – the UCR – on the

---

[23] The PRO was legally recognized as a national party, that is, with the minimum number of affiliates in five or more districts, as of June 3, 2010, that is, after its merger with Recrear.

Table 3 Districts in which the PRO participated in national elections according to labels (2003–13)

	Number of provinces in which the PRO competed under its own visible label	Number of provinces in which PRO joined with allies under other labels (PRO acronym not visible)	Total number of provinces in which PRO participated
2003	1	0	1
2005	3	0	3
2007	7	1	8
2009	8	2	10
2011	3	8	11
2013	7	10	17

Source: Author's own elaboration based on data from the National Electoral Chamber.

way to the nationalization of a competitive center-right electoral option, were crucial for the PRO to establish links with secondary constituencies, allowing it to overcome the social encirclement in which the conservative parties had until then been confined.

The successful incorporation of leaders from traditional parties was possible because the PRO established a division of labor–mechanism that proved effective in solving the problem of horizontal coordination among such a diversified political staff. This mechanism allowed the original ruling coalition to maintain control of the party's electoral strategy and identity, while selective incentives were distributed among ambitious politicians who came to the PRO from traditional political forces. This division of labor made it possible to provide a factor identified by Rosenblatt (2018) as necessary to ensure party vibrancy: namely, the construction of channels for the political careers of its leaders.

The strategy of offering recruited leaders opportunities to satisfy their political ambitions can be seen, for example, in the fact that all different backgrounds were represented among the PRO local deputies and/or city of Buenos Aires government officials: according to my 2011 survey, 14 percent of the people in these positions were former UCR members, 21 percent came from Peronism, 19 percent were conservative leaders, 17 percent came from the business world, and 29 percent from the NGO world. However, some of these groups were more committed to the PRO than were others. Taking formal party membership as a proxy for this engagement, only 14 percent of leaders with a UCR background and 45 percent of leaders with a Peronist background included in my 2011 survey were PRO members, as opposed to 70 percent of the conservative leaders, 66 percent of the businesspeople, and 80 percent of NGO members. One observes a similar pattern of differences in how much time and resources members of the various intraparty groups invested in animating the party's internal life: 53 percent of the NGO cadres and 50 percent of the conservative leaders held party positions, as opposed to 45 percent of the Peronists and 33 percent of the businesspeople who held such positions; no leaders with a UCR background had a party position in the PRO. Involvement in party life was thus lower among those who came from traditional parties, while new politicians and conservative leaders were the ones who invested most in building the PRO organization. The interviewees argued that this lesser degree of involvement on the part of the former is explained, first, by the PRO's ruling coalition's strategy of controlling the internal life of the party as a means to control its political-electoral strategy and brand building. They also attributed it to the fact that politicians from the traditional parties were not willing to identify fully with a nascent party.

This division of labor within the party, accepted by both groups, defined clear roles: the PRO's ruling coalition did not require cadres who came from traditional parties to formally participate in the party's internal life, and instead excluded them from the work of devising party strategy and controlling the party brand. Conversely, in exchange, members of these factions received places on electoral lists and government positions were awarded to leaders only weakly engaged with the party. The data from my 2011 survey of PRO leaders in the city of Buenos Aires allow us to identify the patterns of allocation of positions in the party's electoral lists and appointments to high government positions. Fewer than half (48 percent) of the party members with the highest level of engagement—that is, those serving in leadership roles – were appointed to nonelective positions in government or were ranked highly enough on the party's electoral lists to have a reasonable expectation of winning office (calculated on the basis of the seats obtained by the PRO in the previous election), that is, were given expectant elective positions. By contrast, 90 percent of the cadres with less organizational commitment to the PRO were rewarded for their participation in the party with either appointment to nonelective office (52 percent) or inclusion in the party's electoral lists in an expectant elective position (38 percent).

The analysis of my 2011 survey based on membership of intraparty groups according to background yields similar results. The businesspeople were almost entirely absent from the electoral lists, and those who participated in the lists did so in a manner more symbolic than substantive, because two out of nine of them, in my small sample, occupied nonexpectant positions. Conversely, the former UCR leaders either held nonelective positions (five of seven), or participated in elections with a high expectation of being elected (two of seven). At the same time, the groups most engaged with the party had the highest percentage of cadres competing in elections in expectant positions (four out of ten of the leaders had a background in traditional conservative parties, with four out of fifteen of those coming from NGOs). In Siavelis and Morgenstern's (2008b) typology, the PRO distributed its expectant positions on the electoral lists to those who were party loyalists and entrepreneurs. In Panebianco's (1988) terms, the PRO followed a strategy that combined the distribution of collective incentives (to those leaders most involved with the party) and selective incentives (to the least involved leaders).

The success of this division of labor and the incentive distribution strategy associated with it is also a source of cohesion among party leaders. This cohesion can be seen, for example, in the fact that the PRO survived an electoral defeat in the city of Buenos Aires (2003), its stronghold, and a defeat at the national level in 2019. It also survived its leader's exit from the local scene when Macri was elected president in 2015, and the leader's departure from the center of the party scene after the 2019 election setback.

5 Political Mobilization of Conservative Parties Based on "Moral Panic" and Fear of the "Venezuela Model"

Programmatic renewal and investment in organizational mediations with core constituencies and noncore constituencies required a third element that functioned as a trigger for political and electoral mobilization in support of conservative parties. This third element is a moral incentive for partisan mobilization and is especially effective among those groups that are ideologically and socioculturally closer to the parties. Existing theory focuses on authoritarian contexts as providers of these incentives for political mobilization in parties. According to the ASPs scheme, it is in the context of counterinsurgency wars that conservative sectors find sufficiently solid sources of cohesion to maintain party commitment over time. However, my scheme argues that these sources of cohesion can be obtained in nonauthoritarian contexts where there is intense political conflict and/or polarization. In such contexts, conservative-party builders can tap into the salient fears of their electoral base – mostly associated with redistributive threats and threats to property (Durand & Silva, 1998) – to offer themselves as a political solution to the threat. To do so, conservative leaders associate the threat with the main political adversary, usually a progressive one, and then offer organizational resources – such as close-to-the-party organizations – to channel the energies triggered by this fear toward party support.

This mobilization was effective in cases where economic elites had dispersed electoral attachments (Argentina), and in promoting electoral participation in elective voting countries such as Colombia. This moral incentive consisted of a feeling of urgency and danger in the face of the possibility of the "Venezuela model" – which implies a drift toward political authoritarianism, radical redistribution policies, and economic statism – that is, a threat to property (Durand & Silva, 1998) – spreading to other countries in the region (Gamboa Gutiérrez, 2019; Rovira Kaltwasser, 2019; Vommaro, 2017). The fear of "chavization" thus created moral incentives for certain social sectors to change their level of political involvement and/or their political preferences. Evidence shows that fear also facilitates the mobilization of sociocultural cleavages in polarized societies. The progressive cultural agenda had advanced in the region since the 1980s in some cases. Feminist and LGBT+ demands had gained increasing attention in the public sphere and in legislatures. During the years of the left turn, feminist and LGBT+ movements found favorable political opportunities to advance their agendas. In some cases, these advances triggered a cultural backlash from conservative sectors who mobilized against what they called "gender ideology" (Biroli & Caminotti, 2020). Conservative groups who made a shift toward moderation avoided openly aligning themselves with this backlash. Conservative groups that radicalized programmatically, on the other hand, found a powerful vector of political mobilization in this mobilization based on the fear of normative changes. In their classic work, Lipset and Rokkan (1967) pointed out that disputes about "public morality" function as one of the topics on which political cleavages are based (Levitsky et al., 2016). Thus, to be more effective, cleavages can exploit the mobilization of social fears related to moral threats.

The perception of threats is a crucial factor in the study of elite mobilization and in the birth and growth of conservative parties. However, the political efficacy of these perceived threats has not been studied in relation to the Latin American Right. The presence of moral panic processes in the case of the PRO reveals certain continuities between conservative parties prior to and after the "third wave" of democratization (Huntington, 1991). In a way, this fear of "chavization" reactivated Cold War and anticommunist logics. The fear of communism had been a powerful incentive for the mobilization and unity of conservative partisans in Latin America during the Cold War (Williams, 2017).

Exploiting the fear of chavization was a strategy used by conservative social and political leaders to, in some cases, mobilize their core constituency, and, in others, to expand their electorate. Unlike the radicalization of the Latin American Left in the sixties, which elicited the perceived threat of an expansion of the Cuba model in large part because leftist youth activists identified themselves as *guevaristas*, here it was rather a label affixed by the leftists' adversaries. Thus, since mobilization of moral panic is also a political strategy of mobilization and of discrediting the Right's adversaries, the main thing is that this mobilization strategy, to be effective, had to connect with real fears (of the advance of "gender ideology," of "authoritarianism," of "economic chaos," etc.).

5.1 Mobilize Economic Elites: The PRO and the Strategic Use of Fear of Chavization in Argentina

The moral panic elicited by the Venezuela model acted in Argentina as a moral incentive for the political mobilization of the economic elites in favor of, first, the PRO and, later, the Cambiemos coalition. This panic produced a sense of urgency in the business world by convincing some of the economic elites that it would be necessary to act in the political sphere "before it was too late." In this sense, the Argentine case is a true laboratory in which to study the operation of the moral incentives that facilitate conservative-party mobilization.

Beginning in 2008, and with greater force after 2011, political polarization intensified in Argentina. The year 2008 was when the conflict began between agricultural producers and the then newly initiated Cristina Fernández de Kirchner administration about the official proposal of changing the tax system for grain exports. The government was challenged in the streets and defeated in the legislative arena. It responded by emphasizing the more radical components of its redistributive program and its national-popular antiestablishment discourse, a more clearly state-centered and center-left profile. When Cristina Fernández de Kirchner was re-elected in 2011, these identity components were sharpened and there was a partial replacement of government elites and leadership of official support organizations – which since then have formed the core of the ruling FPV – to the detriment of the traditional Peronist elites. Kirchnerist Peronism increasingly relied on allies with a more clearly populist leftist, or national-popular profile. It also reinforced conflict rhetoric. This happened to coincide with the decline in international commodity prices, and the ensuing scarcity of the resources needed to continue redistributive policies (Campello & Zucco, 2016).

By 2013, the Ministry of Economy was led by a young heterodox economist close to the Kirchnerist group La Cámpora. La Cámpora was the leading Kirchnerist youth group created in 2007 and led by the Kirchners' son, Máximo Kirchner. It was the most solid and mobilized activist base of support for Kirchnerist Peronism and also the most inclined to defend policies of state intervention in the economy. Relations between economic elites and the government became more distant. The government took economic measures to control access to the dollar and to control imports and exports. These measures, taken by politicians outside the business world, were experienced as a threat by economic elites. During those years, a moral panic thus spread throughout the business world regarding the possibility of chavization in Argentina (Vommaro, 2017), that is, a shift to a noncapitalist economy and a non-liberal-republican form of governance. At that traumatic juncture (Rosenblatt, 2018), a strong reaction to Kirchnerist "populism" took place that was organized and politically translated by the PRO. This is consistent with Edward Gibson's argument that "the fortunes of conservative electoral movements in Latin America are negatively correlated to the health and strength of the bourgeois-state relationship. Where a significant rupture in that relationship has taken place, business has mobilized vigorously behind conservative parties and has given impetus to their growth" (1992: 32).

In my interviews with businesspeople who joined the PRO since 2011, this feeling of panic was clearly expressed. "Cristina's last term was terrifying, everything began to be exacerbated," said Francisco, a CEO who later joined the Cambiemos government (Francisco, personal communication, August 18, 2016).[24] In that period, the economic elite began to experience the social and business atmosphere in Argentina as intolerable: "There was this feeling that there are no limits, as if they [the government] said 'let's go for everything.'"[25] Sonia recalls that in 2012, when the Argentine state expropriated 51 percent of the shares of Fiscal Oilfields (YPF), owned by the Spanish company Repsol, she stopped reading newspapers for a while: "I didn't want to read or hear anything," she told me. Respondents mentioned a sense that the government was hostile to them. Comments included:

> "The thing that bothers me the most is the arbitrariness."
> "The acts of authoritarianism revolt me."
> "The arrogance bothers me a lot."
> "The overflow of individual freedoms . . ."
> "They broke the law and it didn't matter, those are the things that drive me out of my mind."
> "In the end, what caused me the most rejection was the feeling of . . . the easy and populist discourse that generated sympathy."

---

[24] Francisco, personal communication, August 18, 2016.
[25] Sonia, manager of a financial company, personal communication, November 21, 2016.

The feeling of fear was activated in relations with government officials. "All the time you felt the presence of the state," said Estela, a lawyer specializing in finance.[26] "There are no limits to the powers of the state [. . .] they use the AFIP [the federal tax agency][27] as a quasi-gestapo to put pressure on citizens or companies," said Néstor, CEO of a financial intermediation company.[28] "It was all slowed down, you couldn't import, they brought the country to a halt," a manager said, who then faced the dilemma of either participating in politics or emigrating.[29] Those in the business world felt a lack of protection. This discomfort sometimes focused on particular leaders in Kirchner Peronism. Comments included:

> "Alberto Fernández [chief of staff of Néstor Kirchner] irritated me especially, he seemed to enjoy [making things difficult for me]."
> "Néstor Kirchner was treating me very badly, he seemed like a guy . . . deeply insolent."
> "He's a gangster."
> "We were totally subjugated."
> "They cause resentment . . ."

The first mass antigovernment protests took place in 2012. These demonstrations were organized by right-wing activists without partisan ties and were led by people from the middle and upper-middle classes. In them, protesters voiced both economic (against dollar access regulations) and institutional demands (against acts of corruption) (Gold & Peña, 2019). The PRO set out to represent those sectors that felt that Cristina Fernández de Kirchner's government was running roughshod over them.

In that context, the fear of chavization worked as a moral incentive for political mobilization. Chavization was the label that the PRO used, consistent with other Latin American conservative parties, to label the fear felt by economic elites and the upper-middle-class social sectors. The strong emotional component of this perception of threat warrants describing it as a panic.

Venezuela was the great enemy of the Latin American Right, but also of the traditional parties in Europe and the United States, including social democrats.[30] Chávez's identification with socialism and his alignment with

---

[26] Personal communication, November 10, 2016.

[27] Administración Federal de Ingresos Públicos (Federal Administration of Public Revenue).

[28] Personal communication, November 8, 2016.

[29] Jean-Pierre, former CEO of an electronic payment instruments company, personal communication, November 15, 2016.

[30] On the differentiation between the "sensible and modern" Latin American Left and a "demagogic and populist" Left, see Ramírez Gallegos (2006).

Cuba had caused many to reject him. But the situation in Venezuela was not part of the daily horizon of worries of ordinary citizens in Argentina. In that country, thus, this moral panic was confined to the economic elites. However, as I pointed out, those elites did not have a permanent link with any political force, not even with the PRO.

In that context, PRO leaders carried out a strategic use of that fear. This strategy had two main components. First, PRO leaders publicly used the argument of avoiding falling into the "Venezuela model" in a systematic way. This argument was wielded to criticize the FPV government's measures during Cristina Fernández de Kirchner's second term and to defend the Cambiemos government's measures as of 2015.[31] Likewise, the Macri administration carried out an aggressive foreign policy toward Venezuela that it linked to its fight against the partners of "chavismo" in domestic politics, that is, Kirchnerist Peronists.[32] At the same time that this threat was used as a discursive strategy of mobilization, the PRO mobilized its organizational resources to offer economic elites channels of mobilization against that threat. Those PRO leaders linked to economic elites implemented organizational efforts to mobilize businessmen through close-to-the-party organizations, such as the G25. The managers, who were already part of the PRO administration in the city of Buenos Aires, functioned as moral entrepreneurs (Becker, 1963), defining the framework of the social problem and convincing their colleagues to engage politically in order to prevent the chavization of Argentina. This sense of urgency was translated into a historical opportunity to participate in a new, market-friendly political party, in which other colleagues were already taking part. Macri's nomination in 2015 then emerged as a way out of that threatening situation. The unanimity of support for Macri from the country's major businessmen can be interpreted as a product of that juncture. In short,

---

[31] For example, in the face of a union conflict involving subway workers in Buenos Aires, Macri, then mayor of the city, stated: "today it is clear to me that she [Cristina Fernández de Kirchner] wants to take Argentine society to a Chavist model of monolithic thinking, wary of those who think differently!" (August 12 2012, available at www.buenosaires.gob.ar/noticias/macri-la-presidenta-quiere-llevar-la-argentina-un-modelo-chavista).

[32] See, for instance, "Los cruces de Macri con Maduro y sus críticas al régimen chavista," *Perfil*, January 24, 2015, available at: www.perfil.com/noticias/politica/como-mauricio-macri-endurecio-su-postura-frente-a-venezuela.phtml. In the same vein, in an interview with the Spanish newspaper *El País*, Macri said: "We Argentines have seen it [the dangers of Chavism] up close because Kirchnerism brought us to the brink of *chaviz-ing* Argentina and we had to fight hard to avoid it. I know what the Venezuelan people are suffering, I believe that what we have to follow is a firm position, without euphemisms [...] We will help where we can to get out of this social, political and economic conflict" (*El País*, February 18, 2017, https://elpais.com/internacional/2017/02/17/argentina/1487352179_836718.html).

the systematic use of the threat as a discursive strategy of moral appeal and the channeling of the threat through close-to-the-party organizations explains why the PRO was able to take advantage of the moral panic of the "Venezuela model" to mobilize economic elites who were reluctant about party engagement.

6 The Interaction between the Three Factors

The three factors identified by my argument were necessary to the success of PRO's party building; taken separately, no one of them is sufficient. Future testing of the model will determine whether the three factors taken together are sufficient. How do the three factors of the model interact? First, throughout this Element I have shown that programmatic renewal favors the establishment of links with noncore constituencies that reinforce the organizational work in this regard. Moderation in cultural or distributive issues can function as a strategy for reaching out to the "average voter" in times of progressive consensus. Selecting issues that are ignored by left-wing political groups but are of great impact on the daily life of citizens, such as security, allows conservative parties to gain relevance in the public eye and to dominate an issue that is salient to a large sector of society. Programmatic innovation reinforces the PRO's recruitment of leaders from traditional parties like the PJ (Partido Justicialista/ Justicialist Party) and the UCR, both of which measures are taken in order for the party not to be confined to the traditional conservative electorate in Argentina, which is numerically small (Gibson, 1996).

Secondly, by establishing close-to-the-party organizational linkages with the core constituency, the Right can obtain a direct benefit from propagation of the idea among the elites that the local Left will follow the "Venezuela model." The close-to-the-party organizations allow the party to channel the fears of the economic elites. This is shown by the PRO case, in which party leaders rooted in the business world circulated testimonies about the situation in Venezuela through a variety of activities, such as talks with Venezuelan opposition politicians. Conversely, a moral panic about chavization reinforced the moral incentives of managers and CEOs to participate in partisan channels of various kinds, from the creation of programs to the supervision of polling stations. Mobilizing the threat gave the party cohesion and purpose, fundamental to cementing a party identity resilient to electoral setbacks and a driver of growth in adverse times (Rosenblatt, 2018), such as those that the PRO faced in the 2019 presidential election.

Finally, the strategic mobilization of a threat reinforces programmatic renewal. In the case of programmatic renewal through moderation, it can offer a counterbalance to the phenomenon whereby hardline supporters are dissatisfied with the adoption of progressive positions on cultural or distributive issues. When the threat is solidly associated with the adversary party, conservative party leaders can always present themselves as the only possible barrier of containment against that absolute evil.

The interaction between the three factors in the model can also produce less efficient outcomes. As noted, threats are central incentives for the mobilization of support but can negatively affect the flexibility of parties in incorporating new demands. In the case of parties that have carried out programmatic moderation, the importance of these threats for supporters' sense of identification with the party can also weaken internal support over time. Parties may lose this flexibility and become rigid in programmatic terms. This can directly affect their relationship with noncore constituencies. Take the case of the PRO in Argentina. Although my model does not seek to explain electoral results, part of the weakening of the party in the 2019 presidential elections had to do with the waning effectiveness of the threat of chavization. In 2019, Peronism presented a moderate candidate, which diminished fear among economic elites. At the same time, the poor economic performance of Macri's administration made his presentation as an alternative to the economic chaos associated with Venezuela less plausible. Finally, the adoption of an orthodox line on economic matters made the PRO more akin to previous doctrinaire right-wing options and made it less audible to less ideological electorates. This programmatic shift was enough to weaken the PRO's ability to attract more centrist, swing voters. In any case, these problems were more critical to the election itself than to my subject here: the ability of conservative parties to achieve centrality in the political system. Under that measure, the PRO continues to be a central party of the Argentine political system, despite its electoral defeat.

Finally, the use of patronage resources to establish relationships with noncore constituencies can negatively affect the programmatic renewal of conservative parties. The PRO presents itself as a pragmatic and efficient problem-solving party. Patronage and clientelism are publicly perceived as negative for the efficiency of public policies. Although the leading coalition of the PRO achieved, through a careful elaboration and control of the party brand, the invisibility of traditional politicians and the links they establish with their electoral clienteles, their opponents' denunciations of their use of public resources for partisan purposes have the potential to weaken support for the PRO among part of its constituency, strengthening the idea that "all politicians are the same."[33]

---

[33] See, for example, the *Pagina/12* newspaper's criticism of the city of Buenos Aires' local government's obliging its employees to carry out proselytizing activities: "Ya investigan las denuncias de empleados porteños obligados a hacer campaña," www.pagina12.com.ar/221306-ya-investigan-las-denuncias-de-empleados-portenos-obligados-

7 The PRO in Comparative Perspective: Recrear, the Child of 2001 that Could Not Grow Up

As we have seen, another conservative party, Recrear, was emerging at more or less the same time as the PRO. Recrear was a coalition between former UCR leaders and provincial conservative parties. It emerged as the most promising conservative party after the 2001–2 crisis, but it went into crisis shortly after its founding. In its formative years, it had more resources than the PRO. Recrear's founding leader, Ricardo López Murphy, is a renowned economist with a long career in the UCR. He comes from a traditional Radical family (his father was a national deputy for the UCR), and he worked as an activist in the Radical university group the Franja Morada (Purple Band). He was an active participant in internal party life in the province of Buenos Aires and twice served as a minister in the Alianza government, first as Minister of Defense (December 1999–March 2001) and then as Minister of the Economy (March 2001). He was also a prominent member of Fundación de Investigaciones Económicas Latinoamericanas (Latin American Economic Research Foundation, FIEL), a neoliberal think tank founded in 1964 that sought to design public policies and influence the state and the public sphere, but had no explicit partisan ties. In the convulsive political context of 2002, Recrear managed to attract most provincial conservative parties and soon became national in scope (Vommaro, 2017). No other party created in the wake of the 2001–2 crisis had generated such a wide following; most, including the PRO, were concentrated in the city and province of Buenos Aires. Although it grew rapidly and came in third place in the 2003 presidential elections, after this promising start Recrear began a steep decline. In the 2003 elections, in a fragmented scenario, López Murphy won more votes than any other non-Peronist candidate (he obtained 16.4 percent of votes). By 2007 he was showing signs of stagnation in electoral terms (López Murphy reduced his electoral share to 1.6 percent in the 2007 legislative elections in the province of Buenos Aires and to 1.4 percent in the 2007 presidential elections). Faced with this situation, a group of party leaders who had been part of López Murphy's close circle challenged him and, through internal elections, managed to wrest control of the party from him. Recrear went into crisis and eventually merged with the PRO in 2010. Many of the small provincial conservative parties that had seen in Recrear the possibility of finally building a competitive conservative party redirected their hopes toward Macri's movement.

In view of this internal defeat, López Murphy abandoned the party he had founded and created another, Convergencia Federal (Federal Convergence). Without the support obtained for Recrear, López Murphy's new group struggled to gain coverage in the country, but nonetheless managed to run in the 2011 elections allied with a small conservative party, the Autonomist Party. López Murphy made a run for the head of the government of the city of Buenos Aires with this party, but performed poorly (1.4 percent of votes).

After that, López Murphy's political participation became erratic and eventually irrelevant. Only in 2021 did he manage to compete in elections again, and he did so allied with the PRO. To a certain extent, this was an acceptance of the victory of his opponent, the other party to have emerged out of the 2001–2 crisis and to have built a successful conservative party. Recrear embarked on a parallel path to that of the PRO under similar conditions. If context is not an effective variable, what explains Recrear's failure?

The reasons can be found in the leaders' decisions and their organizational consequences in relation to the ideational and organizational resources needed to build a conservative party. In the first place, Recrear made a low programmatic innovation. López Murphy had gained public notoriety as a result of his time as the head of the Ministry of the Economy, during the Alianza government. He had proposed severe spending cuts that affected higher education funding, and for that reason he was repudiated by members of his own party, which had seen public universities as a space for financing and activist recruitment. López Murphy had to resign just two weeks after taking office. The crisis that started in December 2001 was interpreted by López Murphy and his group as the result of their not undertaking the necessary cuts at the right time. Like other conservative groups, he blamed Alianza's unwillingness to make those cuts on the "populist" irresponsibility of the traditional parties. In the aftermath of the crisis, some conservative sectors saw López Murphy as a champion of fiscal discipline. He was also presented by these groups as the candidate who could have avoided the crisis by employing austerity policies. This interpretation led to the diagnosis that there was a constituency seeking a political force that clearly defended conservative ideas in the economic sphere. Likewise, the increase of social protest in the streets awakened in these sectors a demand for programmatic proposals clearly identified with the defense of law and order. The testimony of the leaders who were members of Recrear supports this claim. In the words of one of them, "the objective was to look for a center-right constituency. We wanted to fill a gap that was not covered" (National leader and founding member of Recrear, cited in Cruz, 2019: 109).

Certainly, Recrear's leaders was consistent with these positions. Based on the three surveys we conducted on PRO leaders (2011, 2014–15, and 2017), I identified those who came from Recrear to find out whether they had differences in ideological and programmatic terms with those who had other backgrounds. According to my data, former Recrear leaders are located further to the right than PRO leaders with other backgrounds. This small sample of Recrear leaders excludes leaders who decided not to join the PRO in 2010 and therefore has a "less conservative" bias. However, when comparing leaders who came from Recrear and the rest of the PRO, the differences are significant (p-value=0.0125 in the Wilcoxon test) and show that Recrear leaders have an average positioning further to the right.

In any case, these former Recrear leaders accepted the PRO's more moderate program, so we could argue that the absence of programmatic moderation in Recrear was fundamentally due to its party leaders' decision to build an orthodox program in the economic and conservative social sphere rather than the characteristics of its leaders.[34]

Analysis of Recrear's electoral platform in 2003 suggests that Recrear leaders chose a strategy of openly defending the well-known neoliberal ideas of fiscal austerity, tax cuts, and deregulation of labor, financial, and commercial markets.[35] In that manifesto, for instance, Recrear proposed a regime of public financing for basic education based on the charter school model, according to which families would receive a credit and then decide which school to allocate it to, instead of the state's financing public education according to its own criteria. On political and social issues, it followed the discursive pattern of the preceding conservative parties, associated with the defense of the *mano dura* and the repression of social protest. With Cold War language associated with the conservative core, far from the party's centrist constituency, the program argued that it was necessary to choose:

> either the rule of law, or the revolutionary state. Both systems cannot coexist, as it happens nowadays, where leaders of these groups claim the revolutionary right in prestigious television programs, without any prosecutor acting as he should, and are received in the government offices to "negotiate." [36]

In the social field, Recrear's program proposed to remove the Ministry of Social Development, created in 1999, and to eliminate the national conditional cash-transfer social programs that had been implemented to address the

---

[34] Furthermore, we find that there are no significant differences between the positioning of the leaders from Recrear and the rest of the PRO's leaders in relation to the economic, political, and cultural issues of public salience measured in the three surveys and presented in Section 4 of this Element.

[35] In this case, the platform appears to be a good access point to the programmatic decisions of Recrear's leaders, since the role of López Murphy in its elaboration was central. As a party leader recalls, "López Murphy paid a lot of attention to the program. I was in several campaigns and I never saw one where so much attention was paid to the program. He participated directly. There were issue teams, it was presented, it was discussed. And Ricardo was there. He would have been the most informed president of Argentina" (cited in Cruz, 2019: 121).

[36] Recrear's electoral platform, 2003, https://manifesto-project.wzb.eu.

deterioration in the lower classes' living conditions due to the increase in unemployment, underemployment, and informal employment, and in particular the Jefas y Jefes de Hogar Desocupados program (Unemployed Heads of Households program), which had reached a coverage of almost 2 million people. In its place, Recrear proposed the creation of an agency to finance targeted programs at the provincial level, evaluating the allocation of funds on a cost–benefit and case-by-case basis.[37] This severe cut in social spending was proposed in a context in which the country still had high rates of poverty and unemployment. The only national program that Recrear's electoral program proposed to maintain was a project of public financing of private employment.[38]

After that campaign, Recrear maintained the main lines of its discourse. The coalition with the PRO in 2005 could have created incentives for moderation, or at least for selecting nontraditional issues from the conservative electoral offer that would allow Recrear to connect with broader constituencies. However, during the electoral campaign, López Murphy maintained the same hardliner discourse and, after disputes with his PRO allies, he became entrenched in the doctrinaire defense that had given birth to his party. According to some interviewees, López Murphy's refusal to moderate the party program is among the causes of the internal conflict that worsened as of 2007 and ended with López Murphy's resignation from the party that he had founded. The other main point of the conflict was the need to merge the two conservative options behind the PRO, which had managed to gain control of the government of the city of Buenos Aires in 2007. This was what was advocated by a group of young people from Recrear led by Esteban Bullrich, who would later found the G25 Foundation, the close-to-the-party organization that allowed the PRO to recruit economic elites. This group sought to follow the example of the Spanish Partido Popular: It was necessary to have a conservative party that would address a broad constituency, from the center to the right. Finally, this group won the internal election against López Murphy and began the process of merging with the PRO. In López Murphy's Recrear resignation speech in 2008, he defended "doctrinal positions" over "chameleonic parties":

> Recrear was not born to be a chameleonic party adaptable to any ideology, where values, doctrinal positions, and behaviors matter little. We were born to have a precise orientation, beyond what the surveys indicated . . . That was the project that motivated a group of citizens to found Recrear in 2002, in the context of the collapse of the Argentine political system and in view of the need for its regeneration.[39]

---

[37] Recrear's electoral platform, 2003, https://manifesto-project.wzb.eu.

[38] Recrear's electoral platform, 2003, https://manifesto-project.wzb.eu.

[39] Excerpt from the closing speech of the Recrear Leaders Training Course, December 17, 2007, http://rlopezmurphy.blogspot.com/2007/12/cierre-de-cursada-del-curso-de-formacin.html.

On the contrary, when Bullrich took over as president of Recrear, he defended the importance of putting ideas into practice, that is, reaching power, over the purity of doctrine:

> We do not come to hold a rubber stamp, we come to renew and work, because we believe that these ideas should be put into practice, they should be able to represent the majority of citizens. We do not come to be the laughing stock of anyone, we are a group of leaders who believe in a set of ideas and values, but who want to put them into practice. We do not want a testimonial effort . . . we want to be a National Party.[40]

In addition to the difficulties it faced in finding a programmatic appeal and reaching beyond its conservative constituency, Recrear did not invest heavily in building organizational resources, or build close-to-the-party organizations to mobilize and organize its core constituency. Instead, it preferred to individually aggregate some leaders, without offering them clear channels for their ambitions (Rosenblatt, 2018). It incorporated small provincial conservative parties, but did not build internal mechanisms that would integrate these heterogeneous groups and give them levels of coordination and cohesion. The inclusion of Radical leaders was important for electoral know-how, but they were leaders from small cities with weak social roots and small constituencies. Basically, Recrear was a personalist party that depended on the star power of its leader.

Experienced Radical leaders from intermediate cities in the province of Buenos Aires were Recrear's starting point. A study on how Recrear was built (Cruz, 2019) highlights the participation of José María Lladós, a Radical leader and militant from the city of Pergamino in the agrarian center of the province of Buenos Aires; and César Martín García Puente, a leader of the National Line, a conservative faction of the party based in Arrecifes, another district in the agrarian center of the province of Buenos Aires. José María Lladós and García Puente were joined by Manuel Solanet, a neoliberal FIEL economist like López Murphy, based in the city of Buenos Aires. This small group had neither party structure nor social roots, but in some cases, they were long-standing leaders with electoral know-how. In 2002, the party also incorporated some elite lawyers, who sought spaces for participation. As we have seen, the 2001–2 crisis triggered a need to do something for the country among the economic elites. However, Recrear followed a pattern of individual recruitment, without building organizational resources that would allow it to turn this participation into lasting support

---

[40] "Speech to assume the presidency of Recrear," January 5, 2008, https://diputadobullrich .wordpress.com/page/3.

and, at the same time, a basis for new recruits. Fundamentally, the party acted only as a vehicle for López Murphy's ambitions.

Recrear's great organizational advantage was the incorporation of small provincial parties. However, this was carried out in the form of a coalition between parties, without establishing integration and coordination mechanisms. The provincial conservative parties sought to build an electoral option of their own. Before the 2001–2 crisis, some of them had converged in support of the AR party, which collapsed with the severe setback of its leader Domingo Cavallo, the last Minister of Economy of the Alianza government. Cavallo had been identified by a large part of society as responsible for the country's economic crisis, his reputation fell into disrepute and the AR collapsed. The conservative parties that allied themselves with Recrear had social roots in their provinces and, in the most successful cases in electoral terms, they had deputies and senators in the National Congress. However, they did not have a visible leadership and an appealing candidate. The figure of López Murphy appeared, then, as an attractive option for their project of building a unified conservative electoral option.

The organizational amalgamation between the different groups was poor and Recrear did not manage to establish mechanisms to coordinate these leaders of disparate origins. For instance, in the 2003 subnational elections (of governors and national deputies by district) the relationship between the partners followed this disorganized pattern and lacked effective levels of coordination between leaders. Only in three of the country's twenty-four districts did Recrear manage to present unified lists for governor and national deputies. Meanwhile, in five of those twenty-four the coalition partners presented separate lists and competed against each other (Cruz, 2019: 116). On the day of the 2003 presidential elections, after learning that he was not one of the top two most-voted-for candidates and therefore excluded from the second round, López Murphy seemed to take these difficulties into account and told his followers:

> We have to convert this enormous electoral weight, these almost 4 million votes into deputies, senators, mayors, governors, councilmen, we have to make a permanent political force of enormous vigor, and above all finish mending our affections, finish cohesion of this new political space, that is what we are going to dedicate ourselves to.[41]

However, Recrear did not advance in that direction. According to our field-work in Quilmes and Pergamino, districts of the province of Buenos Aires,

---

[41] Speech by Ricardo López Murphy in the RECREAR bunker, April 27, 2003. DiFilm (June 5, 2014). DiFilm – Ricardo Lopez Murphy – Elecciones Presidenciales 2003. Online Video Clip. www.youtube.com/watch?v=YXygTCTkfi0.

Recrear made little organizational progress in its formative years. The presence of the party was articulated in a handful of local leaders of Radical and conservative origins, with little social rooting and without coordination mechanisms among them and between them and the leading coalition of the party, represented by López Murphy and his collaborators. The provincial conservative-party leaders interviewed also pointed out the lack of coordination among the groups that formed Recrear. In particular, they pointed out the enormous autonomy they had in defining the electoral strategy and the candidacies in their districts. This absence of organizational coordination mechanisms prevented Recrear from transforming from a federation of small parties supporting a personalist vehicle to a cohesive and coordinated party (Luna et al., 2021). While López Murphy enjoyed popularity and was an attractive candidate, he managed to control his coalition of support. As he lost that popularity, the allied parties began to look for new partners. The coalition with the PRO in 2005 worked as a "natural" way out for those conservative parties, in view of López Murphy's electoral setback, which became more notorious after 2007. The same happened with newcomers who had joined Recrear in 2002. For them, the experience of the coalition between PRO and Recrear in 2005 was the accurate way to build a solid conservative party with national scope. However, López Murphy was opposed to establishing a permanent alliance with the PRO. Faced with this refusal, the newcomers successfully wrested control of the party away from the leader. Finally, they initiated the merger with the PRO in 2008, which concluded in 2010. A leader of Recrear who had worked with López Murphy said at the beginning of the internal conflict: "We all love and respect Ricardo but we only accompany him to the cemetery gate. Beyond that, no."[42]

Finally, Recrear did not systematically use the Chavist threat as a moral appeal capable of triggering electoral mobilization. Certainly, Recrear went into decline before the political polarization in Argentina intensified and Kirchnerist Peronism took a popular-nationalist discursive turn and began to replace traditional government elites with young loyalists with more clearly redistributive visions. That is to say that Recrear did not count on a favorable context for its party builders to tap into salient fears that could turn into moral panics with possible political effects, associated to a sense of urgency. On the contrary, until 2007, Kirchnerism had had a relatively moderate rhetoric and sought to occupy the political center. In that context, Recrear leaders sought to mobilize their core constituency with the classic antipopulist discourse of conservatives in Argentina, associated with the excessive public spending of

---

[42] See *El Cronista*, November 21, 2007, "Con Murphy fuera de juego, Recrear se alineó con Macri," www.cronista.com/impresa-general/Con-Murphy-fuera-de-juego-Recrear-se-alineo-con-Macri-20071121-0043.html.

Peronist governments. They also used more traditional criticism of Cuba and its allies as a means to defend an orthodox economic approach, but they did not build a narrative of threat and mobilization around these issues. Rather, the appeal was based on "rational" concepts, associated with the evidence that the only programmatically coherent option in economic terms was the one proposed by Recrear. The figure of López Murphy as an economic expert accompanied this framing. Likewise, references to Chávez and the "Venezuela model" did not occupy a central place in López Murphy's discourse. For example, after the Summit of the Americas in the city of Mar del Plata, in 2005, when progressive presidents reached an entente and decided to reject the implementation of a free trade area (FTAA), López Murphy criticized the government for missing opportunities to open markets, without mentioning "chavization" or redistributive threats.[43] In short, Recrear mobilized a fear of left-wing populism in its electoral speeches, but this threat relied on the traditional conservative moral cohesion, effective for the small groups that already supported the party but uncapable of mobilizing hesitant supports.

Conclusions

At the beginning of the 2000s, the study of the organizational forms built by conservative parties in Latin America had received little scholarly attention (Middlebrook, 2000: 290). Since then, a number of authors have advanced our understanding of this subject (Cannon, 2016; Loxton, 2021; Luna, 2014; Rosenblatt, 2018). This Element, based on in-depth empirical work, contributes to these advances. In this final section I propose some comparative reflections to examine how the three factors of my model operate in other cases beyond Argentina. I then make two clarifications about my framework's scope, one concerning the role of leadership in conservative-party building, and the second concerning the specificity of the partisan pathway for conservative groups to gain power and influence. At the end, I offer some comments about the relationship between conservative parties and democracy.

Comparative Implications beyond the Argentina Case

How does my three-factor scheme travel to other cases, beyond Argentina? In Latin America, other conservative parties without authoritarian roots have sought a place in national politics in recent decades. The CD in Colombia, and one of the main Bolivian regional parties, the MDS, managed to develop some of the factors outlined in my model, but in each of these cases, at least one

---

[43] See www.infobae.com/2005/11/09/221480-para-lopez-murphy-se-perdieron-oportunidades-crear-mercados/.

of the factors that explain the success of the PRO is missing.[44] In Colombia, in a more favorable nonauthoritarian context for the birth of conservative parties, the CD managed to gain a foothold in the electoral scene, but was less successful in building organizational resources. Unlike the Argentine case, in Colombia, traditional right-wing parties – the Liberal Party and the Conservative Party – had historically dominated the electoral struggle, excluding leftist competitors through formal and informal arrangements, and successfully survived the challenges of the "third wave" of democratization (Wills-Otero, 2015). Thus, until 1990, the Liberal Party (PL) and the Conservative Party (PC) collectively obtained between 87 percent and 97 percent of the seats in Congress (Botero, Losada, & Wills-Otero, 2016). It was a closed two-party system. However, after the 1991 constitutional reform, new party actors and internal divisions among traditional parties emerged. Toward the end of the 1990s, scholars argued that the country was moving from bipartisanship to a fragmented multiparty system (Botero, Losada, & Wills-Otero, 2016) with low ideological alignment. Traditional parties were weakened in terms of their electoral legitimacy.

The opportunity arose for the emergence of a new political force. Regarding programmatic issues, since the 1970s, issues related to security – both armed conflict and high levels of insecurity and drug trafficking – had come to rank among the greatest public concerns (Botero, Losada, & Wills-Otero, 2016). The traditional parties had no coordinated or permanent position regarding this issue. In the 1990s, policies of dialogue and confrontation with the guerrillas were tested, without success. By 2002, the problem of political violence remained unresolved by conservative and liberal governments, which left space "available" for a new proposal. Alvaro Uribe, a former PL leader from Antioquia, carried out much of the programmatic renewal before constituting a political force. Once Uribe became president in 2002, he consolidated a political brand, supporting this by creating an NGO and later the CD, which served as the custodian of the *uribista* program. One way in which the CD carried out programmatic innovation was by elaborating its own perspective on the issue of internal security and incorporating it into its party brand – "democratic security"; it did so on the basis of radicalization rather than moderation, by proposing an iron-fist approach to Colombia's internal conflict.

---

[44] To outline the CD and MDS's party-building processes, I conducted interviews with key informants (partisan leaders and scholars, in the Colombian case, and scholars in the Bolivian case). I also consulted data from party studies in those countries; these data enabled me to describe these parties' organizational development efforts, their territorial expansion, and their programmatic transformations, as well as their links with associations, NGOs, and other civil-society organizations that were part of their partisan environment.

However, it did not invest in party organization in a sustained manner. The founding leader and main electoral asset of the party, Uribe, discouraged the construction of a locally anchored party structure, as well as the creation of close-to-the-party foundations that in the Argentine case helped to aggregate the interests of the economic elites (on the Chilean case, see Pribble, 2013). Instead, Uribe mobilized traditional local leaders and recruited individuals from the economic elites without creating intraparty or close-to-the-party organizational resources. The CD's personalistic features adopted the pattern that Uribism had followed since its birth in 2002. Uribe was a politician from one of the traditional parties whose career had followed the usual trajectory (he was elected senator and governor in Antioquia running as a PL candidate). In 2002 he wanted to win the PL's nomination for the presidency, but he failed to gain the support of the party apparatus. Dissatisfied, Uribe filed his candidacy under a new party label, First Colombia. Uribe won the 2002 elections in the first round, with 53 percent of the vote. The PC, which had failed to present its own candidate, supported Uribe, as did various liberal groups, including one led by Juan Manuel Santos. At the same time, these groups created an electoral vehicle, the U Party, to support Uribe. The U Party was conceived as an instrument to support the candidacies of first Uribe and then Santos. It had an extremely weak structure and a low programmatic definition, making it difficult to identify its electorate (Botero, Losada, & Wills-Otero, 2016). Uribe only decided to create his own party when, out of office, he had to compete against Santos. There, he mobilized the pre-existing *uribista* networks, formed largely by traditional politicians, and added businesspeople and technocratic cadres. However, the approach continued to be to incorporate small groups and recruit individuals who responded personally to the leader, without building coordination mechanisms among them. Thus, the CD grew as a party dependent on the figure of Uribe, who is also inseparable from the party brand (Gamboa Gutiérrez, 2019). Although it would not be impossible for it to become a success story in the future, so far it is uncertain how it will cope with the departure of its leader from the scene and whether it will manage to build organizational resources that will give it resilience to setbacks of different kinds – such as poor performance by the government, or an electoral defeat.

Finally, Uribe and the other CD leaders strategically rode the threat of "Castrochavismo" against both the peace agreements (2016) and the rise of a competitive electoral Left (represented by Gustavo Petro in 2018). They also succeeded in associating this threat with conservative groups' fear of the advance of the progressive agenda on gender issues; in this, it was unlike the PRO which, in a context of broad consensus in favor of the expansion of sexual and gender rights, especially in the city of Buenos Aires where the party was born, chose the path of moderation in this field. The term Castrochavismo remained in the public arena, mobilized by Uribe and the leaders of the CD as a moral incentive to support their proposals. The fact that, between 2014 and 2018, three elections –the 2014 and 2018 presidential elections and the 2016 plebiscite – were influenced by the cleavage around the peace process contributed to the continued currency of the term (Pizarro, 2018; Rodríguez-Raga, 2017). The CD case supports what was found in the PRO case: To be efficient, the use of the threat has to be systematic and continuous over time. At the same time, this case shows the need to develop the three factors of my model for the success of conservative parties. Without strong organizational resources, the CD remains a case whose success is still uncertain.

The Bolivian MDS was the most solid attempt to build a conservative party at the national level (Otero, 2015) since the debacle of the ADN (Cyr, 2017) and the rise of MAS (Movimiento al Socialismo/Movement Toward Socialism) to power in 2006 (Anria, 2018). Its leader and founder, Rubén Costas, brought together conservative factions and small regional parties in the richest area of the country, the Media Luna, in eastern Bolivia. Mobilizing these groups, Costas led the government of the department of Santa Cruz for more than a decade. However, Costas and the other MDS leaders failed to build a national party (Eaton, 2016; Zegada Claure, 2019). In 2021, the MDS had no competitive candidate and had to support another conservative leader, Luis Fernando Camacho, who had gained visibility in the institutional coup against Evo Morales in 2019. Camacho won the election, while the MDS lost its subnational stronghold and went into crisis. The failure of the MDS can be explained by the absence, or weak development of organizational and ideational party resources. In programmatic terms, the transitory decline of the regional cleavage left the conservative program without legs to stand on. Costas did not manage to build a new social groundswell of support for the national launch of his party, nor did he find an issue on which he could build an attractive party brand. In organizational terms, MDS leaders did not invest in intraparty or close-to-the-party organizations to recruit militants and activists and build links with its core constituency and with secondary constituencies. Moreover, Costas' choice of a personalistic approach to party building prevented him from offering career growth channels for ambitious politicians who could contribute to building new social bases. The MDS also did not have a propitious context in which to obtain organizational resources through short-cuts, such as incorporating pre-existing organizations. By the time the MDS was formed, the main grassroots conservative organization in the region, the Pro Santa Cruz Movement, had been weakened after the failure of violent protests against Evo Morales; its main leaders had been discredited or imprisoned, or had gone into exile (Eaton, 2007). The MAS agreement with the Santa Cruz economic elites required that the latter abandon the political scene in exchange for economic concessions (Farthing, 2019). After having contributed funding and other forms of direct support of the autonomy movement, economic elites chose to stop investing in organization building (Eaton, 2011). The agreement also weakened the CPSC (Comité Pro Santa Cruz/Santa Cruz's Civic Committee) and other grassroots conservative movements, as their support from the business sector also dissipated. Both phenomena weakened the support of the MDS in its core constituency (Eaton, 2016). Finally, after a mobilization of the threat of the "Venezuela model" in the early years of the Morales government (Stefanoni, 2007), Morales' agreement with the economic elites defused the recourse of appealing to fear of the leftist party in power to mobilize the conservative electoral base. With the failure of the MDS, in Bolivia to date, since the ADN debacle, it has not been possible to build a national conservative party (Eaton, 2016).

My argument provides an explanation for the success or failure of conservative parties born in nonauthoritarian contexts in Latin America, that is, after democratic transitions, which contributes to fill the gap in the ASPs theory. Future research should test its applicability in other regions where conservative parties emerge in contexts relatively distant from past authoritarian experiences, such as Eastern or Southern Europe.

The Influence of Political Leaders

My model focuses on the efforts of party leaders to build ideational and organizational resources in the contexts in which they operate. The decisions of party builders have a direct impact on the construction of party mechanisms that reproduce these resources over time. However, my argument is not leader-centered, but party-organization-centered. In some interpretations of conservative parties' rise in Latin America, an exclusive focus on leadership prevails. It is argued that attractive personalistic appeal explains the success of the conservative parties, as in the case of Macri in Argentina or, in electoral terms, Uribe in Colombia. Undoubtedly, individual leadership is essential for understanding the construction of the Right in the region (Cannon, 2016). In general, effective leadership has been identified as a key factor in party building (Van Dyck, 2014), both because it enables a party to create a competitive electoral offer based on a candidate's appeal and because it helps create internal cohesion in the newly created party (Levitsky, Loxton, & Van Dyck, 2016). Other works also highlight leadership capacity as the cause of successful or failed party adaptation, as occurred in social democratic parties in Spain, France, and Italy

(Kitschelt, 1994) or in communist parties in the postcommunist era (Grzymala-Busse, 2002).

The partisan cases studied in this volume are all strongly based on personalistic leadership. The PRO grew electorally around Macri and was organized around him. Leaders constitute a fundamental political asset for new parties (Cyr, 2017) by virtue of their popularity and their electoral appeal. They put their stamp on the party brand and make strategic decisions related to the construction of that brand. They function as faction assemblers, especially when the party incorporates ambitious politicians who come from traditional political parties. For instance, they function as referees for intraparty conflicts (Morresi & Vommaro, 2014). However, the approval of leaders is fragile and subject to the ups and downs of popularity. When parties do not manage to build ideational and organizational resources that do not depend only on that foundational leader, they are more exposed to any setbacks that individual figure might encounter. This is what happened with Recrear, a vehicle built around López Murphy's leadership. Conversely, the PRO built up ideational and organizational resources that allowed it to overcome electoral setbacks and, especially, the defeat of its leader in the 2019 presidential election.

In other words, party leaders matter, and matter a great deal, but to build successful conservative parties these leaders must build party resources (both ideational and organizational) and reproduce these over time. They must also maximize the resources available to their parties by making strategically appropriate decisions at critical moments (Cyr, 2017). Uribe's opposition to building solid organizational resources for the CD weakened his party's resilience. The personalist approach also weakened the MDS, which ended up in crisis after Costas' exit from the electoral scene. It is beyond the scope of this Element to identify the factors that explain leaders' ability to use these resources competently, but this issue will undoubtedly be addressed by future research.

Rights, Power, and Electoral Pathways

The partisan route is probably the costliest way in the short term for conservative groups to achieve power and influence. Certainly, it is possible to build competitive electoral vehicles, and even to win elections, without developing political parties (Luna et al., 2021). This is especially true for right-wing movements, which historically had the financial, organizational, and symbolic resources needed to intervene politically in different ways. Meanwhile, conservative groups have other organizational forms beyond the parties, and use other strategies to influence governments and to access the state (Luna & Rovira Kaltwasser, 2014). Think tanks, media conglomerates and lobbying, and direct personal contacts with the rulers (Viguera, 1996), but also religious networks and exclusive membership clubs form part of the Right's organizational repertoire in the region (Cannon, 2016). These organizations compete not only for influence over the orientation of public policies, but also to define the model of society that should prevail in the country: the influence of economics in the social world, the embeddedness of "entrepreneurial culture," and so on.[45] The influence of conservative intellectual cadres in military governments in Argentina (Morresi, 2015), as well as the management of economic policies in Pinochet's Chile by the Chicago Boys (Huneeus, 2016) illustrate these other paths to power (Luna & Rovira Kaltwasser, 2014) which, in fact, have been the most common paths in the recent history of conservative forces (Gibson, 1992: 31). The different paths are not exclusive; on the contrary, they have overlapped in the past (Middlebrook, 2000).

However, the phenomenon of successful conservative parties in a context where instances of successful party building are rare (Levitsky et al., 2016) needs to be explained. In this Element, I explain it in terms of the political work of organizing and mobilizing different social and economic groups. In order to be competitive, the conservative actors I have considered invested in party organization at some point on their path. Investment in party organization, whether formal or informal, implies establishing stable links both with the party's core constituency and with its noncore constituencies. The investment in party organization yields coalitions that have durability over time. I am, thus, interested in the constituency building carried out by these parties that enabled them to mobilize the conservative-related groups that, until then, had only influenced the government by nonpartisan means.

Some studies claim that conservative parties are the direct expression of elites (Cannon, 2016). Without denying the clear connection between them, here I am interested in the partisan mobilization of those elites, and in the factors that favor it. In this sense, I do not see parties as mere reflections of pre-existing cleavages and interests. Rather, I am interested in parties' agency oriented to build ties with the social worlds from which they obtain activist, discursive, and aesthetic repertoires (Vommaro, 2017). These social worlds define the party's core constituency. In order to build these ties with core constituencies, ambitious leaders act as mobilizers in organizational terms, and as interpreters in programmatic terms (Han, 2014).

---

[45] I could mention here the activism on the part of NGOs and foundations linked to the promotion of ideas, such as think tanks (Freedom Foundation, etc.), but also foundations associated with the development of entrepreneurship, such as Junior Achievement, as well as religious foundations associated with the defense of conservative views of sexuality and gender relations.

Conservative Parties and Democracy

In normative terms, the development of competitive conservative parties was associated with greater democratic regime stability, because conservative parties channeled interests that might otherwise turn to authoritarian approaches (Middlebrook, 2000; Ziblatt, 2017). When conservative groups have a successful conservative party to support, they have fewer incentives to adopt authoritarian means to gain power (Coppedge, 2000). The institutional coup in Bolivia in 2019 and the situation in Venezuela during the era of Chavismo seem to be consistent with this argument. In both cases, conservative groups did not have competitive parties with which to challenge the governing Left and, in the face of authoritarian drift by these leftist governments, the right-wing forces preferred the path of institutional destabilization. By contrast, in Argentina, as well as in Chile and Uruguay, conservative parties managed to defeat the governing Left by electoral means, which must be counted among the factors that explain the relatively peaceful transfer of power in those countries, which had strong authoritarian traditions.

Non-ASP parties, moreover, have the virtue of not drawing their source of cohesion from the counterinsurgency war. Their main resources do not come from authoritarian contexts, so their commitment to democracy seems earned. However, some features of the development of conservative parties in non-authoritarian contexts can create problems for the task of consolidating democracy. First, cases of programmatic renewal toward more extreme positions, such as the Colombian case, show that conservative parties can also use – or at least tolerate – violent means of controlling opponents. In that country, since 2016, 543 social leaders have been killed in circumstances related to conflicts over land ownership (Prem et al., 2018). Also, in the 2019 municipal elections, at least forty-five candidates received death threats from armed actors. Although it is not possible to hold the CD directly responsible for this violence, the CD leader, Uribe, makes criminalizing statements about social leaders, especially indigenous people, and has opposed the Duque administration's dialogue with them in response to protests. A hardline security position can thus conspire against a democratic life in which civil and political rights are fully realized.

Second, as I said above, the strong reactionary component that contains the moral incentive for the mobilization of conservative parties produces a type of electoral representation that, in order to preserve its vitality, requires the perpetuation of a stereotyped image of its political adversary. This image can justify forms of political repression, manipulation of justice, and other authoritarian methods. Piñera's repressive reaction to student mobilizations in 2011 and to the 2019 citizen mobilizations shows the low tolerance that conservative parties have for collective protest action and for the mobilization of social demands that are not easily assimilated by their programs. Demonstrations carried out by lower-class organizations and social movements are quickly labeled as a threat and discounted as efforts by the "enemy camp." Piñera chose to talk about a "war" when he was facing the most important social mobilization of Chilean society since the beginning of the current democratic cycle (Pribble, 2019). Macri's reaction to opponents of his pension reform in 2017 followed this pattern (Vommaro, 2019). In addition, a governing conservative party will often encounter difficulties establishing agreements with the opposition, because any settlement would contradict one of the primary incentives that mobilized its own adherents, namely the rejection of the opposition based on fear. This construction of the adversary as an object that elicits panic can also encourage forms of conservative mobilization that, when the Right is out of power (i.e., when it is in opposition) can cause political instability. In short, the existence of successful conservative parties is a necessary, but not sufficient, condition for a vital democratic competition that respects the civil and political rights of citizens.

References

Alessandro, M. 2009. Clivajes sociales, estrategias de los actores y sistema de partidos: la competencia política en la Ciudad de Buenos Aires (1995–2005). *Revista de la Sociedad Argentina de Análisis Político* 3(4): 581–614.

Anria, S. 2018. *When Movements Become Parties: The Bolivian MAS in Comparative Perspective*. New York: Cambridge University Press.

Barndt, W. T. 2014. Corporation-Based Parties: The Present and Future of Business Politics in Latin America. *Latin American Politics and Society* 56 (3): 1–22.

Becker, H. 1963. *Outsiders: Studies in the Sociology of Deviance*. New York: Free Press.

Beisel, N. 1990. Culture, and Campaigns against Vice in Three American Cities, 1872–1892. *American Sociological Review* 55(1): 44–62.

Biroli, F., & M. Caminotti. 2020. The Conservative Backlash against Gender in Latin America. *Politics & Gender* 16(1): E1.

Blee, K. M., & K. A. Creasap. 2010. Conservative and Right-Wing Movements. *Annual Review of Sociology* 36: 269–286.

Botero, F., R. Losada, & L. Wills-Otero. 2016. Sistema de partidos en Colombia 1978–2014: ¿La evolución hacia el multipartidismo? In F. Freidenberg (ed.), *Los sistemas de partidos en América Latina: Cono Sur y Región Andina*. Mexico City: Instituto Nacional Electoral (INE), pp. 339–400.

Bril Mascarenhas, T. 2007. El colapso del sistema partidario de la ciudad de Buenos Aires: una herencia de la crisis argentina de 2001–2002. *Desarrollo Económico* 47(187): 367–400.

Burgess, K. 2003. Explaining Populist Party Adaptation in Latin America: Environmental and Organizational Determinants of Party Change in Argentina, Mexico, Peru, and Venezuela. *Comparative Political Studies* 36 (8): 881–911.

Calvo, E. 2005. Argentina, elecciones legislativas 2005: consolidación institucional del kirchnerismo y territorialización del voto. *Revista de Ciencia Política* 25(2): 153–160.

Campello, D., & C. Zucco. 2016. Presidential Success and the World Economy. *The Journal of Politics* 78(2): 589–602.

Cannon, B. 2016. *The Right in Latin America: Elite Power, Hegemony and the Struggle for the State*. New York: Routledge.

Cohen, S. 1972. *Folk Devils and Moral Panics: The Creation of the Mods and Rockers*. London: MacGibbon and Kee.

Coppedge, M. 1998. The Dynamic Diversity of Latin American Party Systems. *Party Politics* 4(4): 547–568.

Coppedge, M. 2000. Venezuelan Parties and the Representation of Elite Interests. In K. J. Middlebrook (ed.), *Conservative Parties: The Right and Democracy in Latin America*. Baltimore, MD: Johns Hopkins University Press, pp. 110–136.

Cruz, F. 2019. *Socios pero no tanto: Partidos y coaliciones en la Argentina. 2003–2015*. Buenos Aires: Eudeba.

Cyr, J. 2017. *The Fates of Political Parties: Institutional Crisis, Continuity, and Change in Latin America*. New York: Cambridge University Press.

Di Tella, T. S. 1971–2. La búsqueda de la fórmula política argentina. *Desarrollo Económico* 11(42/44): 317–325.

Durand, F., & E. Silva (eds.). 1998. *Organized Business, Economic Change, and Democracy in Latin America*. Miami, FL: North-South Center Press.

Eaton, K. 2007. Backlash in Bolivia: Regional Autonomy as a Reaction against Indigenous Mobilization. *Politics & Society* 35(1): 71–102.

Eaton, K. 2011. Conservative Autonomy Movements: Territorial Dimensions of Ideological Conflict in Bolivia and Ecuador. *Comparative Politics* 43(3): 291–310.

Eaton, K. 2016. Challenges of Party-Building in the Bolivian East. In S. Levitsky, J. Loxton, B. Van Dyck, & J. I. Domínguez (eds.), *Challenges of Party-Building in Latin America*. New York: Cambridge University Press, pp. 383–411.

Echt, L. 2020. Think tanks partidarios: conocimiento para política pública o activismo político? *Revista de la Sociedad Argentina de Análisis Político* 14(1): 75–103.

Farthing, L. 2019. An Opportunity Squandered? Elites, Social Movements, and the Government of Evo Morales. *Latin American Perspectives* 46(1): 212–229.

G25. 2013. *Anuario 2013*. Buenos Aires: Area de Comunicación y Diseño de G25.

G25. 2014. *Anuario 2014*. Buenos Aires: Area de Comunicación y Diseño de G25.

Gamboa Gutiérrez, L. 2019. El reajuste de la derecha colombiana: el éxito electoral del uribismo. *Colombia Internacional* 99: 187–214.

Garay, C. 2016. *Social Policy Expansion in Latin America*. New York: Cambridge University Press.

Gibson, E. L. 1992. Conservative Electoral Movements and Democratic Politics: Core Constituencies, Coalition-Building, and the Latin American Electoral Right. In D. Chalmers, M. de Souza, & A. Boron (eds.), *The Right and Democracy in Latin America*. New York: Praeger-Greenwood, pp. 13–42.

Gibson, E. L. 1996. *Class and Conservative Parties: Argentina in Comparative Perspective*. Baltimore, MD: Johns Hopkins University Press.

Gidron, N., & D. Ziblatt. 2019. Center-right political parties in advanced democracies. *Annual Review of Political Science* 22: 17–35.

Gold, T., & A. M. Peña. 2019. Protests, Signaling, and Elections: Conceptualizing Opposition-Movement Interactions during Argentina's Anti-Government Protests (2012–2013). *Social Movement Studies* 18(3): 324–345.

Grandinetti, J. 2015. "Mirar para adelante": tres dimensiones de la juventud en la militancia de Jóvenes PRO. In G. Vommaro & S. Morresi (eds.), *"Hagamos equipo": PRO y la construcción de la nueva derecha argentina*. Buenos Aires: Ediciones de la UNGS, pp. 231–263.

Grzymala-Busse, A. M. 2002. *Redeeming the Communist Past: The Regeneration of Communist Parties in East Central Europe*. New York: Cambridge University Press.

Han, H. 2014. *How Organizations Develop Activists: Civic Associations and Leadership in the 21st Century*. New York: Oxford University Press.

Holland, A. C. 2013. Right on Crime? Conservative Party Politics and *Mano Dura* Policies in El Salvador. *Latin American Research Review* 48(1): 44–67.

Huneeus, C. 2014. *La Democracia Semisoberana: Chile Después de Pinochet*. Santiago de Chile: Taurus.

Huneeus, C. 2016. *El Régimen de Pinochet*. Santiago de Chile: Taurus.

Hunter, W. 2010. *The Transformation of the Workers' Party in Brazil, 1989–2009*. New York: Cambridge University Press.

Huntington, S. 1991. *The Third Wave: Democratization in the Late Twentieth Century*. Norman, OK: University of Oklahoma Press.

Kessler, G. 2009. *El sentimiento de inseguridad: sociología del temor al delito*. Buenos Aires: Siglo XXI Editores.

Kitschelt, H. 1986. Political Opportunity Structures and Political Protest: Anti-nuclear Movements in Four Democracies. *British Journal of Political Science* 16(1): 57–85.

Kitschelt, H. 1994. *The Transformation of European Social Democracy*. New York: Cambridge University Press.

Landau, M. 2018. *Gobernar Buenos Aires: ciudad, política y sociedad, del siglo XIX a nuestros días*. Buenos Aires: Prometeo.

Levitsky, S. 2001. Inside the Black Box: Recent Studies of Latin American Party Organizations. *Studies in Comparative International Development* 36 (2): 92–110.

Levitsky, S. 2003. *Transforming Labor-Based Parties in Latin America: Argentine Peronism in Comparative Perspective*. New York: Cambridge University Press.

Levitsky, S., & K. M. Roberts (eds.). 2011. *The Resurgence of the Latin American Left*. Baltimore, MD: John Hopkins University Press.

Levitsky, S., J. Loxton, & B. Van Dyck. 2016. Introduction: Challenges of Party-Building in Latin America. In S. Levitsky, J. Loxton, B. Van Dyck, & J. I. Domínguez (eds.), *Challenges of Party-Building in Latin America*. New York: Cambridge University Press, pp. 1–48.

Levitsky, S., J. Loxton, B. Van Dyck, & J. I. Domínguez (eds.). 2016. *Challenges of Party-Building in Latin America*. New York: Cambridge University Press.

Lipset, S. M., & Rokkan, S. 1967. Cleavage Structures, Party Systems, and Voter Alignments: An Introduction. In S. M. Lipset & S. Rokkan (eds.), *Party Systems and Voter Alignments*. New York.: The Free Press, pp. 1–64.

Loxton, J. 2016. Authoritarian Successor Parties and the New Right in Latin America. In S. Levitsky, J. Loxton, B. Van Dyck, & J. I. Domínguez (eds.), *Challenges of Party-Building in Latin America*. New York: Cambridge University Press, pp. 245–272.

Loxton, J. 2021. *Conservative Party-Building in Latin America: Authoritarian Inheritance and Counterrevolutionary Struggle*. Oxford: Oxford University Press.

Luna, J. P. 2010. Segmented Party-Voter Linkages in Latin America: The Case of the UDI. *Journal of Latin American Studies* 42(2): 325–356.

Luna, J. P. 2014. *Segmented Representation: Political Party Strategies in Unequal Democracies*. Oxford: Oxford University Press.

Luna, J. P., R. Piñeiro, F. Rosenblatt, & G. Vommaro. 2021. Political Parties, Diminished Subtypes, and Democracy. *Party Politics* 27(2): 294–307.

Luna, J. P., & C. Rovira Kaltwasser (eds.). 2014. *The Resilience of the Latin American Right*. Baltimore, MD: Johns Hopkins University Press.

Lupu, N. 2016. *Party Brands in Crisis. Partisanship, Brand Dilution, and the Breakdown of Political Parties in Latin America*. New York: Cambridge University Press.

Mainwaring, S. (ed.). 2018. *Party Systems in Latin America: Institutionalization, Decay, and Collapse*. Cambridge: Cambridge University Press.

Mainwaring, S., & T. Scully (eds.). 1995. *Building Democratic Institutions: Party Systems in Latin America*. Stanford, CA: Stanford University Press.

Mangonnet, J., M. V. Murillo, & J. M. Rubio. 2018. Local Economic Voting and the Agricultural Boom in Argentina, 2007–2015. *Latin America Politics and Society* 60(3): 27–53.

Middlebrook, K. J. (ed.). 2000. *Conservative Parties, the Right, and Democracy in Latin America*. Baltimore: Johns Hopkins University Press.

Morresi, S. 2015. "Acá somos todos democráticos": el PRO y las relaciones entre la derecha y la democracia en la Argentina. In G. Vommaro & S. Morresi (eds.), *"Hagamos equipo": PRO y la construcción de la nueva derecha argentina*. Buenos Aires: Ediciones de la Universidad Nacional de General Sarmiento, pp. 163–201.

Morresi, S., & G. Vommaro. 2014. Argentina: The Difficulties of the Partisan Right and the Case of Propuesta Republicana. In J. P. Luna & C. Rovira Kaltwasser (eds.), *The Resilience of the Latin American Right*. Baltimore, MD: The Johns Hopkins University Press, pp. 319–342.

Niedzwiecki, S., & J. Pribble. 2018. Social Policies and Center-Right Governments in Argentina and Chile. *Latin American Politics and Society* 59(3): 72–97.

Offerlé, M. 1987. *Les partis politiques*. Paris: Presses Universitaires de France.

Ostiguy, P. 2009. *Argentina's Double Political Spectrum: Party System, Political Identities, and Strategies, 1944–2007*. Notre Dame, IN: Kellogg Institute, University of Notre Dame, Working Paper 361.

Otero, X. M. R. 2015. Bolivia: puntos críticos de las elecciones departamentales. *Más poder local* (22): 24–26.

Panebianco, A. 1988. *Political Parties: Organization and Power*. Cambridge: Cambridge University Press.

Pérez Betancur, V., R. Piñeiro Rodríguez, & F. Rosenblatt 2019. *How Party Activism Survives: Uruguay's Frente Amplio*. Cambridge: Cambridge University Press.

Persello, A. V. 2007. *Historia del radicalismo*. Buenos Aires: Edhasa.

Pizarro, E. 2018. Colombia: un tsunami politico. *Nueva Sociedad* 276: 13–23.

Prem, M., A. F. Rivera, D. A. Romero, & J. F. Vargas. 2018. *Killing Social Leaders for Territorial Control: The Unintended Consequences of Peace*. Working Paper 218. Bogotá: Universidad del Rosario.

Pribble, J. 2013. *Welfare and Party Politics in Latin America*. Cambridge: Cambridge University Press.

Pribble, J. 2019. Chile's Crisis Was Decades in the Making. *Financial Times, 29*.

Ragin, C. C. 1994. *Constructing Social Research*. London: Pine Forge Press.

Ramírez Gallegos, F. 2006. Mucho más que dos izquierdas. *Nueva Sociedad* 205: 30–44.

Rodríguez-Raga J. C. 2017. Colombia: país del año 2016. *Revista de Ciencia Política* 37(2): 335–367.

Rosenblatt, F. 2018. *Party Vibrancy and Democracy in Latin America*. Oxford: Oxford University Press.

Rovira Kaltwasser, C. 2019. La (sobre)adaptación programática de la derecha chilena y la irrupción de la derecha populista radical.*Colombia Internacional* 99: 29–61.

Sawicki, F. 1997. *Les réseaux du Parti socialiste: sociologie d'un milieu partisan.* Paris: Belin.

Scarrow, S. E. 2000. *Parties without Partisans: Political Change in Advanced Industrial Democracies.* New York: Oxford University Press.

Schneider, B. R. 2004. *Business Politics and the State in 20th Century Latin America.* New York: Cambridge University Press.

Seawright, J. 2012. *Party-System Collapse.* Stanford:, CA Stanford University Press.

Seawright, J. & J. Gerring. 2008. Case Selection Techniques in Case Study Research: A Menu of Qualitative and Quantitative Options. *Political Research Quarterly* 61(2): 294–308.

Stefanoni, P. 2007. Siete preguntas y siete respuestas sobre la Bolivia de Evo Morales. *Nueva Sociedad* 209: 46–65.

Stokes, S. 2001. *Mandates and Democracy: Neoliberalism by Surprise in Latin America.* New York: Cambridge University Press.

Tavits, M. (2013). *Post-communist Democracies and Party Organization.* New York: Cambridge University Press.

Torre, J. C. 2003. Los huérfanos de la política de partidos Sobre los alcances y la naturaleza de la crisis de representación partidaria. *Desarrollo Económico* 42 (168): 647–665.

Van Dyck, B. 2014. Why Party Organization Still Matters: The Workers' Party in Northeastern Brazil. *Latin American Politics and Society* 56(2): 1–26.

Van Dyck, B. 2021. *Democracy Against Parties: The Divergent Fates of Latin America's New Left Contenders.* Pittsburgh, PA: University of Pittsburgh Press.

Viguera, A. 1996. La acción política de los empresarios en América Latina. *Ecuador Debate* 38: 167–196.

Vommaro, G. 2017. *La Larga Marcha de Cambiemos.* Buenos Aires: Siglo XXI Editores.

Vommaro, G. 2019. De la Construcción Partidaria al Gobierno: PRO-Cambiemos y los Límites del "Giro a la Derecha" en Argentina. *Colombia Internacional* (99): 91–120.

Vommaro, G., & M. Armesto. 2015. ¿Nuevos políticos en el partido, viejos políticos en las listas? Reclutamiento partidario y división del trabajo político en PRO, en la Ciudad Autónoma de Buenos Aires. *Pasado Abierto: Revista del CEHis* 1(2): 110–132.

Vommaro, G., & M. Gené. 2022. Policy Legacies, Sociopolitical Coalitions, and the Limits of the Right Turn in Latin America: The Argentine Case in Comparative Perspective. *Latin American Politics and Society* 64(1): 47–71.

Vommaro, G., & S. Morresi. 2014. Unidos y diversificados: la construcción del partido PRO en la CABA. *Revista SAAP* 8(2): 375–417.

Vommaro, G., S. Morresi, & A. Bellotti. 2015. *Mundo PRO*. Buenos Aires: Planeta.

Williams, M. E. 2017. Revisiting the Cold War in Latin America. *Latin American Research Review* 52(5): 916–924.

Wills-Otero, L. 2015. *Latin American Traditional Parties, 1978–2006. Electoral Trajectories and Internal Party Politics*. Bogotá: Ediciones Uniandes.

Wodak, R. 2015. *The Politics of Fear: What Right-Wing Populist Discourses Mean*. London: SAGE.

Zegada Claure, M. T. 2019. El escenario boliviano en 2018: estabilidad económica e incertidumbre institucional. *Revista de ciencia política (Santiago)* 39(2): 147–164.

Ziblatt, D. 2017. *Conservative Parties and the Birth of Democracy*. New York Cambridge University Press.

Acknowledgments

This book reflects more than a decade of research on conservative-party build-ing in Latin America in general, and on the case of the PRO in Argentina in particular. Back in 2009, at the Universidad Nacional de General Sarmiento in Argentina, I began to design a brief research project with Sergio Morresi, which eventually took on major proportions. Several students and young researchers collaborated in this project and took part in the collective book we published in 2015, *Hagamos Equipo* (Let's make a team). Throughout the different stages of our research, we received funding from the National Agency for Scientific and Technological Promotion and the National Council for Scientific and Technical Research (CONICET) in Argentina. From this experience the Grupo de Estudio en Sociología Política (GESP) also emerged, at the Escuela Interdisciplinaria de Altos Estudios Sociales (EIDAES), Universidad Nacional de San Martín (Interdisciplinary School of Higher Social Studies, National University of San Martín). Since 2015, this has been a vibrant and stimulating space for research presentation and intellectual exchange.

This long-term research benefited from invaluable exchanges with colleagues who I admire and respect. With some of them, I discussed some of the excerpts from this Element. Their valuable contributions are reflected in the Element's achievements, but are in no way attributable for its shortcomings. My gratitude goes to Santiago Anria, Martín Armelino, Jennifer Cyr, Hélène Combes, Sebastián Etchemendy, Mariana Gené, Alfredo Joignant, Gabriel Kessler, Juan Pablo Luna, and Vicky Murillo (also two of the editors of the Cambridge Elements series, Politics and Society in Latin America), Martin Paladino, Rafael Piñeiro, Fernando Rosenblatt, Cristóbal Rovira Kaltwasser, Carlos Meléndez, and their colleagues at the Universidad Diego Portales Social Sciences Seminar, Laura Wills Otero and Stéphanie Alenda. I would like to extend my appreciation to them for their contributions to the vibrant discussion on parties and activism in Latin America, and hope that this Element will form a part of that discussion.

Much of this book was also written during the hardest moments of the COVID-19 pandemic, which filled many lives with suffering. That this work is finally in the hands of readers is proof that I am still alive.

That is why my love and gratitude go to Gabriela and Jano, always present in every moment of my life.

Cambridge Elements ≡

Politics and Society in Latin America

Maria Victoria Murillo

Columbia University

Victoria Murillo is Professor of Political Science and International Affairs at Columbia University. She is the author of *Political Competition, Partisanship, and Policymaking in the Reform of Latin American Public Utilities* (Cambridge, 2009). She is also editor of *Carreras Magisteriales, Desempeño Educativo y Sindicatos de Maestros en América Latina* (2003), and co-editor of *Argentine Democracy: the Politics of Institutional Weakness* (2005). She has published in edited volumes as well as in the *American Journal of Political Science*, *World Politics*, and *Comparative Political Studies*, among others.

Tulia G. Falleti

University of Pennsylvania

Tulia G. Falleti is the Class of 1965 Endowed Term Professor of Political Science, Director of the Latin American and Latino Studies Program, and Senior Fellow of the Leonard Davis Institute for Health Economics at the University of Pennsylvania. She received her BA in Sociology from the Universidad de Buenos Aires and her Ph.D. in Political Science from Northwestern University. Falleti is the author of *Decentralization and Subnational Politics in Latin America* (Cambridge University Press, 2010), which earned the Donna Lee Van Cott Award for best book on political institutions from the Latin American Studies Association, and with Santiago Cunial of *Participation in Social Policy: Public Health in Comparative Perspective* (Cambridge University Press, 2018). She is co-editor, with Orfeo Fioretos and Adam Sheingate, of *The Oxford Handbook of Historical Institutionalism* (Oxford University Press, 2016), among other edited books. Her articles on decentralization, federalism, authoritarianism, and qualitative methods have appeared in edited volumes and journals such as the *American Political Science Review*, *Comparative Political Studies*, *Publius*, *Studies in Comparative International Development*, and *Qualitative Sociology*, among others.

Juan Pablo Luna

The Pontifical Catholic University of Chile

Juan Pablo Luna is Professor of Political Science at The Pontifical Catholic University of Chile. He received his BA in Applied Social Sciences from the UCUDAL (Uruguay) and his PhD in Political Science from the University of North Carolina at Chapel Hill. He is the author of *Segmented Representation. Political Party Strategies in Unequal Democracies* (Oxford University Press, 2014), and has co-authored *Latin American Party Systems* (Cambridge University Press, 2010). In 2014, along with Cristobal Rovira, he co-edited *The Resilience of the Latin American Right* (Johns Hopkins University). His work on political representation, state capacity, and organized crime has appeared in the following journals: *Comparative Political Studies*, *Revista de Ciencia Política*, the *Journal of Latin American Studies*, *Latin American Politics and Society*, *Studies in Comparative International Development*, *Política y Gobierno*, *Democratization*, *Perfiles Latinoamericanos*, and the *Journal of Democracy*.

Andrew Schrank

Brown University

Andrew Schrank is the Olive C. Watson Professor of Sociology and International & Public Affairs at Brown University. His articles on business, labor, and the state in Latin America have appeared in the *American Journal of Sociology*, *Comparative Politics*, *Comparative Political Studies*, *Latin American Politics & Society*, *Social Forces*, and *World Development*, among other journals, and his co-authored book, *Root-Cause Regulation: Labor Inspection in Europe and the Americas*, is forthcoming at Harvard University Press.

Advisory Board

About the series

Latin American politics and society are at a crossroads, simultaneously confronting serious challenges and remarkable opportunities that are likely to be shaped by formal institutions and informal practices alike. The Elements series on Politics and Society in Latin America offers multidisciplinary and methodologically pluralist contributions on the most important topics and problems confronted by the region

Cambridge Elements ≡

Politics and Society in Latin America

Printed in the United States
by Baker & Taylor Publisher Services